MW01115582

AWESOME
LVIV

Interesting things you need to know

2nd edition

Kyiv
Osnovy Publishing
2018

УДК   908(477.83-25Львів)(036)=111
Л89

Authors of Awesome Ukraine series — Anna Kopylova, Dana Pavlychko
Executive Editor — Svitlana Libet
Researchers — Anna Protsuk, Ostap Slyvynsky
English Editors — Kim Fraser, Maria Kachmar, Tamara Krawchenko
Photo Editors — Anna Lysiuk, Oleksandra Kiryanova
Copy Editor — Ashton Osmak
Cover illustration — Zukentiy Gorobiyov
Design and layout — Dmytro Ermolov, Anna Kopylova
Printing — Biznespoligraph

Osnovy Publishing
Heorhyivsky provulok 7,
3rd Floor
Kyiv, Ukraine
01030
osnovypublishing@gmail.com
www.osnovypublishing.com

ISBN 978-966-500-670-1

Intro

Lviv is a city whose charm speaks to your senses. It is a city of coffee drinkers, leisurely strolls and bizarre restaurants. The city's somewhat faded grandeur, strong artistic and literary traditions invite a new urban vibe.

Lviv has been at the crossroads of East and West throughout the past eight centuries since its' founding. You can get lost amongst Lviv's ancient churches and synagogues, meander within the Austro-Hungarian Art Nouveau city centre and Soviet-era Modernist apartment blocks.

With this book we are pleased to share with you our love of Lviv! The book is neither a guide nor a manual. Rather, it's an insight into the city we adore — wonderful, fascinating and strange. In its pages you'll find references to major historical events, famous and talented residents, art, culture, sports, literature, traditions and even beloved street food.

CONTENTS

HISTORY

CULTURE

FOOD

HISTORY

*Abraham Hogenberg, **Lviv Skyline**, XVI-XVII cent.*

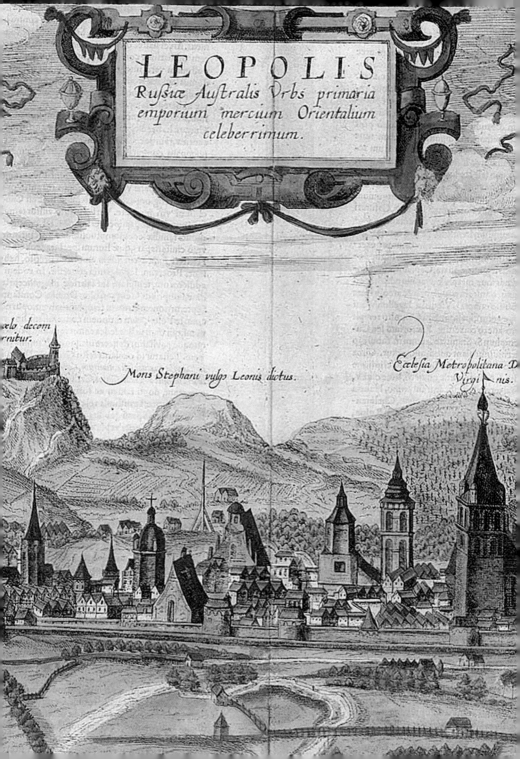

LEOPOLIS

Russiæ Australis Vrbs primaria
emporium mercium Orientalium
celeberrimum.

elo decom
nitur.

Mons Stephani vulgo Leonis dictus.

Ecclesia Metropolitana D
Virgi nis.

King Danylo

King Danylo was the first king of Rus' who founded Lviv in the middle of the 13ᵗʰ century

King Danylo Romanovych of Halych was the ruler of the principality of Galicia-Volhynia (Halychyna-Volyn), a medieval Rus' state bordered by Kyivan Rus' and Poland.

He was a talented ruler who managed to unite the Western Ukrainian lands. As a result, Galicia-Volhynia became the largest state in Europe at the time. At one point, it even included the Kyivan principality with its capital in Kyiv.

Forced to confront the Mongol-Tatar invasions, Danylo of Halych sought alliances with Western Europe. In 1253, he accepted a crown from the Pope of Rome and became the first king of Rus'.

King Danylo established five new cities during his rule, including Lviv, which he named after his eldest son, Lev. Lev later inherited the throne and established Lviv as the new capital.

Though the city never changed its name, it was altered linguistically during different historical periods depending on whose control it was under. Thus, Lviv was known as Lwów in Polish, Lemberg in Ger-

The city's highest point, the High Castle, has gained a practical function in recent years, as it is now the place where a high TV tower stands, which is visible from many parts of the city

The name of Danylo Halych's son Lev translates to "lion", and *this animal became the city's symbol*. More than four thousand pieces of artwork portraying lions have survived to the present day in Lviv

Left: **Coat of arms of Galicia-Volhynia** (1119–1349)
Above: **Stamp, Daniel of Galicia's Cavalier**, XIII cent., Postal History of Ukraine set, 2004

man, Leopolis in Latin, and Lvov in Russian.

At that time Lviv was quite multicultural, as it was inhabited by Germans, Jew, Armenians, Tatars, Saracens and Rusyns/Ruthenians (the former name for Ukrainians). Each ethnicity had its own area of the city. Today, the names of some city centre streets reflect this time period, such as "Virmenska" (Armenian Street), "Staroyevreiska" (Old Jewish Street) and "Rus'ka" (Rus/Ruthenian Street).

The High Castle was a strong fortification on Lviv's tallest hill. The castle was meant to be King Lev's residence, but was deemed unsuitable due to strong winds. Therefore, a new residence, the Low Castle, was built in the valley.

The High Castle was destroyed several times during battles. Both castles were destroyed in the early 19th century.

Today, a mound on the site of the former fortress, which offers a magnificent view of the city, is called the Vysokyi Zamok (High Castle) or Zamkova Hora (Castle Hill).

2

Casimir the Great

In 1340, Polish King Casimir III the Great conquered the Ruthenian (Ukrainian) city of Lviv. This marked the beginning of the Polish period of Lviv's history

Casimir the Great was an ambitious ruler who greatly expanded the borders of the Polish kingdom. He became the first Polish monarch to obtain the title "King of Rus'".

It was during his second campaign for Lviv in 1349 that he managed to annex the city. This marked a new stage in Lviv's development.

King Casimir built a new fortress for himself atop the High Castle, as the previous one had been burnt down during battles.

Casimir the Great invited German engineers and builders to construct the city. They built new Gothic-style walled neighbourhoods, styled after existing fortified German cities. Gradually the German settlers, who were mostly men, assimilated into the Slavic culture by marrying the local Ruthenian (Ukrainian) women.

In the 1360s, Casimir the Great built *a tower on the city's main church*, now the Latin Cathedral. The construction plan envisaged two towers, however, the second one is still unfinished

In 1356, King Casimir granted Lviv *the Magdeburg rights*. Until the end of the 18th century, Lviv remained a self-governing city controlled by an elected city council

*Left: Marcello Bacciarelli, **Portrait of King Casimir the Great**, 1768–1771*
Above: Casimir the Great allowed Gregory, the Armenian Bishop, to stay in Lviv and conduct business there. The document was signed with the royal seal on February 3, 1367

According to one of Lviv's first historians, "the arrows of the Ruthenian Amazons" pierced the hearts of the German warriors.

While Lviv had been a part of the Polish political realm since the middle of the 14th century, Polish culture became dominant in the city only 200 years later. Many Poles who had fled from the failed harvest in central Poland arrived in the city in 1551. Little by little, Polish became the language of clerical correspondence, trade and culture in Lviv.

Polish remained the most popular language in Lviv both during the Habsburg rule and Polish independence between the two World Wars. The Polish era in Lviv ended only in 1939 with the city's annexation to the Soviet Union, along with the rest of the Western Ukrainian lands. It should be noted that throughout these periods, the towns and villages around Lviv were inhabited by a majority Ukrainian speaking population.

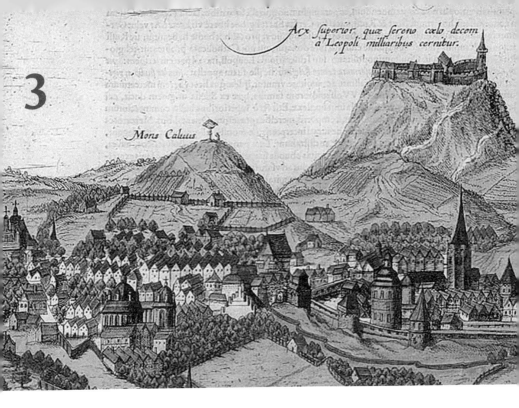

Mons Caluus

Arx superior, quæ sereno cælo decem
a Leopoli milliaribus cernitur.

3

The Brewery Fire

In 1527, medieval Lviv was completely destroyed by the worst fire in the city's history

The Fire of 1527 was Lviv's largest and most significant fire. It was a turning point after which almost nothing of Gothic Lviv remained. The city was completely rebuilt with mainly stone buildings in the Renaissance style.

The fire started in one of the city's breweries. Due to a strong wind, it quickly spread across the city centre.

The buildings that had wood floors and were covered mostly with shingles burnt to the ground completely. Only a few buildings survived, including the Armenian Church and the Town Hall. At the time of the fire, the city gates had been closed, but luckily they were opened quickly enough for most of Lviv's citizens to escape the blaze.

ns *Stephani* vulgo *Leonis dictus.*

Ecclesia Metropolitana DEIparæ Virgi nis.

Eccles

Since the whole city **had been destroyed**, the local government considered moving Lviv to a different location

Only one residential building **survived the fire** due to its having been covered with tiles

Some traces of Lviv's Gothic past *can still be seen today:* in its basements, its pointed first floor vaults, and the rear wall of the Latin Cathedral

Abraham Hogenberg, **Lviv Skyline**, *XVI-XVII cent.*

Military weapons, firearms, bullets and powder kegs, which had been stored in the city's towers, melted or exploded. This resulted in a horrible thunder-like sound that could be heard around the city.

During the reconstruction process, most of the new buildings were built by Italian architects and craftsmen. They were known by such names as Paul of Rome or Peter of Italy.

Of all Ukraine's cities, Lviv has retained the largest ensemble of Renaissance architecture. Some buildings have since been rebuilt, while others still look as though they had been transplanted from Italy, such as the Merchant's Palace on #6 Ploshcha Rynok.

4

Fortress-Monasteries

Medieval Lviv had to constantly defend itself from military incursions. Thus, the city had two lines of defense, the "High Walls" and the "Low Walls". The monasteries surrounding the city centre formed the third line of defense

During medieval times, representatives of numerous Catholic Orders and Eastern Churches regularly arrived in Lviv with the intention of doing missionary work. A densely built city centre could not accommodate everyone. Therefore, monks built their churches and monasteries outside the city walls. In doing so, they had to take responsibility for not only the defense of their monasteries but also for the routes of approach to the city.

Thus, without the existence of any special plan, a unique ring of fortified sacred facilities appeared, located mostly on the ramparts. By the middle of the 18th century, that ring included 46 monasteries and cathedrals. The monasteries successfully defended themselves many times in battles. They also managed to maintain the safety of the residents of the suburbs who were vulnerable to the attacks.

Several monasterial complexes that look like small fortifications have survived to this day. A remark-

Left: Hlyniany Gate, **Bernardine monastery***, 1975–1990*
Above: Monks of St. Onuphrius monastery, Lviv, 2015

Underneath Lviv's historical Old Town is a system of **underground tunnels** connecting the High Castle and the fortified monasteries to each other and the city centre, which was also critical for the defense of the city. According to historians' estimates, only a tenth of all the tunnels built have been discovered to date. Some of them, mostly centuries-old basements located underneath churches, can be seen as part of the "Underground Lviv" tours

St. George Cathedral, the mother church of Ukrainian Greek Catholics, was also built like a fortress on St. George Hill back in Old Rus' times. It was the second highest point after the High Castle in the city's urban landscape. Most of the fortifications have not survived

as the cathedral was rebuilt in the Rococo style in the second half of the 18th century. However, one can still discern its former defense functions in the arrangement of its buildings and **the impregnable slopes surrounding the cathedral**

able example of a fortress-monastery is the St. Onuphrius Monastery on #36 Khmelnitskyi St., founded back in the 13th century, which was subsequently rebuilt several times, and fortified by a strong wall in the 17th century. The Renaissance Benedictine convent on #2 Vicheva Square has also preserved its fortress-like forms. The Barefoot Carmelites and Reformed Christian monasteries and convents, with their baroque temples and fortifications, have also partially survived to this day and can be found on #22 and #30 Vynnychenka St. and #1 Kryvonosa St. The ascetic looking St. Lazarus Cathedral on #27 Kopernyka St. is also still located behind a high wall.

Franz Joseph I

Many Lvivites consider the Austro-Hungarian period a peaceful and prosperous era when you didn't need to cross any borders to get from Lviv to the Adriatic Sea

Emperor Franz Joseph I was one of the most democratic European monarchs. During his rule of almost 70 years, he managed to maintain unity and control over the Great Empire inhabited by more than 25 nationalities. Even during the periods of political turbulence, the Danube monarchy provided a fairly high level of personal freedoms and significant autonomy to its regions.

In 1772, the Galician lands, including the city of Lviv, were annexed to the Austrian Empire. After this, the city developed rapidly; the medieval fortifications were dismantled and secular institutions were set up in churches and monasteries. Many

Emperor Franz Joseph I visited Lviv several times. In honour of his 1851 visit, Zamkova Hora (Castle Hill) was named after him

Under the patronage of Franz Joseph I, a *major Galician Provincial Exhibition* took place in Lviv in 1894

Juliusz Kossak, **Emperor Franz Joseph at the ball in the city hall Lviv**, 1881

government officials from Vienna moved to Lviv and German became the official language. Lviv became the capital of the Kingdom of Galicia and Lodomeria, one of the Empire's provinces. The local parliament, the Galician Sejm, was established.

During the rule of Franz Joseph I, Lviv was transformed into a modern European city. Among the developments were passages for shopping, two large theatres, street lighting, a telephone service, a tramway and a new rail link with Vienna. Residents of Lviv strived to follow the latest Viennese trends and tendencies in everything from architecture to arts and crafts, fashion, cultural life, and technical innovations.

Nostalgia for Austro-Hungarian times, which prevailed in Lviv and Galicia both in the interwar Polish period and in the Soviet era, has become a *part of the tourist image of the city today*. There are many restaurants and coffee shops in Lviv aiming to reproduce the atmosphere of the former Austro-Hungarian Empire. One of the most famous is the "Under the Blue Bottle" coffee shop on #4 Rus'ka Street

Andrey Sheptytskyi

Andrey Sheptytskyi (1865–1944) became the spiritual leader of Galician Ukrainians. while promoting reconciliation between different cultural groups and religions in Galicia

Since the late 17th century, Lviv has been one of the most important centres of the Ukrainian Greek Catholic Church, recognizing the primacy of the Pope of Rome while observing the Eastern rite. After World War II, when the Soviet regime banned the Ukrainian Greek Catholic Church, the church also became a symbol of anti-totalitarian resistance.

Count Andrey Sheptytskyi was the son of a Polonized Ukrainian aristocrat father and a Polish mother, and the grandson of the famous Polish playwright Aleksander Fredro. Sheptytskyi made a very conscious choice in adopting the Ukrainian Greek Catholic religion and the Ukrainian national identity. Although he obtained a degree in law, he decided instead to become a monk of the Eastern rite, having received a blessing from the Pope of Rome to undertake this path. In 1901, he was enthroned as the Metropolitan of Galicia.

Sheptytskyi took responsibility and care for the development of spiritual and social life in Western Ukraine. Not only highly educated,

Archangel Michael, XIV-XV cent., **Crucifixion with Bystanders**, XV cent., **Savior in Glory**, XVI cent.

Andrey Sheptytskyi had a talent for icon painting, and he also had one of the largest icon collections in Europe. This collection became the basis for the Ukrainian National Museum founded in Lviv by Sheptytskyi, located at *#20 Prospekt Svobody*

During World War II, Sheptytskyi helped Jews by offering them shelter in his monasteries and convents and by providing them with forged documents. The Metropolitan personally *saved several hundred Jews*, mostly children

Metropolitan Andriy was an ascetic, content with simple food and old clothes. He used to say *"I eat what my people eat"*

he was also wealthy and he financially supported many social initiatives. He founded a theological research society and the Theological Academy in Lviv, initiated ecumenical congresses as a place of discussion for representatives of different Christian confessions, and he built a hospital and provided broad assistance to orphans and the needy. He also sponsored educational societies, provided scholarships to Ukrainian artists to study abroad, and supported the development of art education. Sheptytskyi also cared for nature and the environment. He founded the Land Bank in Lviv and was vocal in his support for the preservation of cedar forests.

Metropolitan Andriy opposed violations committed by the Soviet regime after the occupation of Western Ukraine in 1939. From the beginning of the German occupation in 1941, he took a strong stance against Nazism. He died of influenza. Count Andrey Sheptytskyi will be remembered for his extraordinary wisdom and selfless commitment to serving others.

7

Death Tango

The circumstances of the "Death Tango" were one of the most tragic and heartbreaking occurrences in Lviv during World War II

After the German occupation of Lviv in June of 1941, the local conservatory and philharmonic were dissolved. The Nazis arrested and imprisoned most of the musicians, mainly Jews, in the in Janowska/ Yanivskyi concentration camp on the outskirts of Lviv.

One of the Nazi SS officers, former nightclub violinist Richard Rokita came up with the idea of organizing a camp orchestra made up of the imprisoned Jewish musicians. The orchestra included the greatest musicians of Lviv, including music professor and conductor Leon Striks and composer and violinist Jakub Mund.

During the day, the orchestra was ordered to play music during executions. At night, they were told to play under the

One of the prisoners, a camp office worker, secretly took a photo of the camp orchestra, which later became famous. He *paid his life for this photo* and the orchestra was ordered to play near his hanged body

balcony of Gustav Willhaus, the camp's Commandant, who was a music lover. They were ordered to compose and perform a special melody for mass executions by gunshot. Nobody knows what this music sounded like or who its composer was, but most presume it was conductor Leon Striks. The piece was called the "Death Tango".

Shortly before the camp was liquidated in November of 1943, the Nazis slaughtered the whole orchestra. Witnesses testified that during the last performance of the "tango of death", each member of the orchestra was ordered to the centre of a circle, told to put their instrument on the ground, stripped, and then shot. The conductor was the last to be shot.

The Janowska/ Yanivskyi concentration camp existed for two years, during which the Nazis *killed between 50,000 and 200,000 people*

8

Stepan Bandera

Stepan Bandera is one of the most divisive figures in Ukrainian history. For many Ukrainians, he is a patriotic hero and a symbol of the struggle for Ukraine's independence. Others disagree with his supposed ultra-right radicalism, considering him a fanatic

Stepan Bandera (1909–1959) was a Ukrainian politician, ideologist and leader of the radical wing of the Organization of Ukrainian Nationalists (OUN).

Born into a patriotic family, Stepan Bandera was a member of the "Plast" Ukrainian Scout Organization in his youth. After graduating from high school he decided to study agriculture and therefore moved to Lviv where he enrolled in the department of agronomy of the Higher Polytechnic School. But before his fi-

nal examination, he was arrested by the Polish authorities of Galicia, for his participation in the Ukrainian national movement. After that he fully devoted himself to political activities.

In the 1930s, as the leader of the OUN, Stepan Bandera turned the OUN's militancy against members of the Polish authorities. In particular, under his leadership, Polish Interior Minister Bronisław Pieracki was assassinated after being accused of anti-Ukrainian policies.

Soviet propaganda created the *myth of the "violent banderivtsi"*, which included any Western Ukrainian patriots who longed for Ukrainian independence. Interestingly, even to this day, Russian propaganda still uses the loaded term banderivtsi to refer to Ukrainian patriots, in the hopes of discrediting them. Ukrainians generally perceive the myth of the "banderivtsi" ironically, while honouring members of the national liberation struggle of the past

In 2004, Bandera was awarded the title of *'Hero of Ukraine'* under the presidency of Viktor Yushchenko. However, it was cancelled by court rule after several years of heated discussions

One of Lviv's longest downtown streets *is named after Stepan Bandera* and a monument, in his honour, was erected in Lviv in 2007

A few days after the German occupation of Western Ukraine, the Bandera-led OUN proclaimed Ukrainian statehood in Lviv and raised the Ukrainian flag atop the Lviv city hall. Hitler subsequently ordered the immediate suppression of this initiative. As a result, Bandera was arrested and imprisoned in the Sachsenhausen concentration camp. Two of Bandera's brothers were tortured to death in Auschwitz.

Bandera survived his 2 ½ year imprisonment in the camp and after the war he returned to political activities. He fled to Austria and Germany. From there he tried to coordinate the UPA underground anti-Soviet armed resistance in Western Ukraine, which lasted until 1954.

In the last years of his life, Bandera and his family were pursued by the Soviet intelligence forces and had to change their place of residence several times. He died in Munich in 1959 at the hands of a Soviet agent who shot him in the face with a potassium cyanide solution.

Viacheslav Chornovil

A journalist by profession and an oppositionist by spirit, Viacheslav Chornovil was one of the most prominent activists and main creators of the independent Ukrainian state

Viacheslav Chornovil (1937–1999) was a politician, journalist, Soviet political prisoner and leader of the democratic liberation movement in Ukraine in the 1980s and 1990s. After graduating from Taras Shevchenko National University of Kyiv, he took a position at the Lviv TV studio as the editor of youth programs.

Chornovil's ideological conflict with the Soviet regime began when he was not accepted into a master's program due to his political convictions, despite the fact that his thesis was already almost completed. His father was also persecuted by the authorities.

In the mid-1960s, when the Ukrainian anti-Soviet dissident movement was just emerging, Chornovil, on several occasions, publicly stated his opposition to the arrests of the intellectuals in the opposition camp and wrote critical articles on the issue. In 1966, he was sentenced to forced labour for the first time. Overall, Viacheslav Chornovil spent about 17 years in Soviet prisons and labour camps.

In 1985, Chornovil returned to

*Protest next to Ivan Franko monument, Lviv, 7th of July, 1988. **Proclamation of Ukrainian Helsinki Union.** Photo from the book "Ukrainian Helsinki Union. 1988–1990 presented by photos and documents"*

Having returned to Lviv after his *imprisonment in labour camps*, Chornovil was only allowed to work in the field of manual labour. He took jobs at the railway station, as a stoker and a weigher

Lviv from his last remote exile. He maintained his oppositional stance while issuing underground publications and advocating for the protection of human rights.

In 1988, Ukraine's first anti-Soviet demonstration took place in Lviv. It was brutally dispersed by the police and became known as "Bloody Thursday". During the demonstration, Chornovil proved himself as a charismatic speaker. That same year, he initiated the creation of the Ukrainian Helsinki Union, the first anti-Soviet political organization in Ukraine.

During the collapse of the Soviet Union, Chornovil co-founded and then headed the most powerful democratic political party in Ukraine — "Narodnyi Rukh of Ukraine" (The People's Movement). In the first Ukrainian presidential elections, he ran for the presidency and came in second to Leonid Kravchuk.

In 1999, Chornovil died in a car crash, the circumstances of which still remain obscure.

CULTURE

Nataliya Halushko-Aksyonenko, **Mask of vertep**, *1995*

Hayivky

At Easter-time, age-old games and songs welcoming the spring are practiced. Seeing them, you might wonder if you've stepped back in time

Every spring during the Easter holidays, Lviv's open-air museum, Shevchenkivs'kyi Hai, hosts fascinating folklore festivities. The entire city dresses up in traditional costumes and heads off to play traditional games, to sing ritual songs, to dance on the green grass, and to watch kozaks sparring and folk competitions.

Historically, hayivky were pre-Chritian Slavic songs to welcome the spring and celebrate the beginning of the agricultural season. Sometimes they are also called vesnianky or "spring songs". Nowadays, hayivky have become an integral part of Christian Easter celebrations. This is a way to feel the fullness of life after the long Lenten season, and an opportunity to come out into the sun after a long winter.

A special part of Easter celebrations is meeting up with friends to share Easter foods, such as paska and krashanky. Paska is special sweet Easter bread and krashnanky are hard-boiled, dyed single-coloured eggs. Both are among the foods blessed in the Easter basket

The day after Easter is called *Oblyvanyi Ponedilok (Wet Monday)*. On this day, it is customary for young men to chase and douse female passers-by with water. Girls may sometimes give the boys a krashasnka to bribe their way out of the trouble or to thank them for being purified by the water. In recent years, this tradition has grown into massive water fights in Lviv. If you are not ready for a cold shower in Lviv's centre, you should avoid crowded places on this day

The vyshyvanka, *a traditional embroidered shirt*, if not a whole national costume, is popular festive attire for Lvivites. They wear vyshyvankas for religious, state or private celebrations, for various ceremonial events at schools and offices, or just for a Sunday stroll in Lviv's city centre

and eaten at Easter. Another of Ukraine's ethnographic trademarks is the pysanka, another dyed Easter egg, which has traditional patterns applied with wax. Each region of Ukraine has its own distinctive colours and patterns for pysanky, just as with embroidery.

11

Christmas Celebrations

The Christmas season in Lviv is very special, with the practice of age-old traditions, bright festivities and the Lvivites' sincere joy at the birth of God's Son

Lviv's small Roman Catholic population celebrates Christmas on December 25th. However, most Lvivites belong to the Eastern Rite Catholic or Orthodox Church and celebrate Christmas on January 7th.

Traditionally, Christmas Eve dinner can only begin once the first star has appeared in the sky. Then families partake in 12 traditional Lenten dishes. Most Ukrainians place a didukh, a sheaf of wheat, in the corner of the house to symbolize abundance, prosperity and the presence of forefathers.

Public celebrations begin on January 7th with family walks, parties and the singing of koliadky — carols. The carols might be ancient, religious, or playful folk songs.

The goat is one of the central characters of the *traditional Old New Year's performance*. Someone in a goat costume is walked from house to house. This is where the modern slang expression, "to walk the goat", originates, which refers to pub hopping in Lviv.

The most popular Ukrainian New Year's carol is Shchedryk, created by *Ukrainian composer Mykola Leontovych* in 1919. It is known worldwide as the *Carol of the Bells*

Carolers in traditional Ukrainian costumes go from house to house, where they are thanked for their songs and poems with money and sweets. You might see some groups perform a vertep, based on the nativity, walking together and holding a colourful Christmas star.

January 14th marks the Old New Year (on St. Malanka and St. Basil day). New Year's songs, called shchedrivky, are sung. They are more secular in nature and were traditionally sung to "invite" spring to arrive. These pre-Christian traditions remain deep-rooted in Ukrainian culture.

On January 18th, Lvivites celebrate Shchedryi Vechir, the Bountiful Evening with a family supper. On January 19th — the Epiphany — priests bless water and the boldest celebrants plunge into the icy waters of frozen rivers and lakes. This date marks the official end of the holiday season, though the atmosphere of joy and fun reigns in Lviv until the end of the month, with holiday concerts and festivals.

Ivan Fedorovych

Ivan Fedorovych (1510(?)–1583) is a founding
father of Ukrainian printing

He created many "first prints" in
Ukrainian, as well as other Eastern
Slavic languages.

Fedorovych (back then his last
name was pronounced in Russian
fashion — Fedorov) began his craft
in the Kremlin, in Moscow's first
printing house. By some accounts,

he was forced to immigrate to
Ukrainian lands because of fierce
book printing competition from
local manuscript copiers.

Ivan Fedorovych issued the first
prints of "Psalter" (1570), "Apostle"
(1574), "Ostroh Bible" (1581), the
East Slavic "Primer" (1574) and many

Acts and Epistles of the Apostles (the "Apostle"), completed in 1574, is the *first Ukrainian printed publication* that has an exact date

Fedorovychych's autograph from July 23, 1583

other texts. These texts were of huge significance to Ukrainian and European history and culture.

You will come across Fedorovych's name often in Lviv, where he lived and worked for many years. The Ukrainian Printing Institute and one of Lviv's central streets were named in his honour. Lviv's biggest second-hand book market is situated near the monument to Ivan Fedorovych (13 Pidvalna Street). Rare books in Ukrainian, Polish and Russian can be found there.

13

Ioann Pinzel

He is called the Ukrainian Michelangelo, though why compare?

This incredible sculptor from Halychyna is a unique figure in world art. Pinzel's life and creative path are shrouded by many unsolved mysteries. It is known that he lived and worked in the 18th century in several cities of Western Ukraine, but the years of his birth and death are unknown and the very name of this sculptor is spelled differently across various archives. Pinzel's sculptures tend to be carved out of wood and are created in the late Baroque tradition. They are considered masterpieces by art historians and are compared with the most outstanding works of the European masters of this epoch. Characteristic features of Pinzel's style are his sculptures' extreme expression and dynamism — the faces of his subjects are often rife with anguish and pain.

In 2012 an exhibition of this outstanding sculptor's best work was held at the Louvre.

In Ukraine, the biggest collection of Ioann Heorh Pinzel's work can be found in the Lviv Art Gallery. The city of Buchach also holds many of Pinzel's works.

Left: *Samson Tearing Apart the Lion's Jaws*, from the altar at the Hodovytsia village cathedral, 1760s. The Museum of Sacral Baroque Sculpture (From the Musuem of Ioann Heorh Pinzel)
Right: *Crucifixion*, from the altar at the Hodovytsia village cathedral, 1760s. From the Musuem of Sacral Baroque Sculpture (The Museum of Ioann Heorh Pinzel)

*Photographs from the book **The Mystery of Pinzel**
by Vira Stetsko, Master Knyg Publishing House, 2013*

Franz Xaver Mozart

The youngest son of Wolfgang Amadeus, Franz Xaver is known as "the Lviv Mozart". This talented pianist and composer brought his European musical experience and culture to Lviv

Franz Xaver was barely five months old when Wolfgang Amadeus died, but the shadow of his father's genius loomed large over him during his entire life (1791–1844). Growing up in Vienna, he became a fine pianist and performed there to great acclaim. But he was plagued with a feeling that he was always going to be compared unfavourably with his brilliant father, and he became discouraged.

At the age of seventeen, in an effort to seek his own identity, he accepted the proposal of a Polish aristocrat to give music lessons to his children on an estate in Galicia.

This was far from the stresses of his life in Vienna and the pay was good, but the young musician found the provincialism of life in small Galician towns to be depressing. Therefore, in 1811, he moved to the more metropolitan Lviv.

Once there, Franz Xavier Mozart immediately set about organizing the city's musical life. He created the Choir of St. Cecilia, which eventually could boast 400 voices. In 1826, the choir gave its first concert in Lviv at St. George's cathedral, in memory of Wolfgang Amadeus Mozart. At this concert, the choir performed

Left: Mozart`s **Lacrimosa** *Liszt piano reduction*
Right: Alexandre Cabanel **"La Contesse De Keller"**, *1989 , Musee d`Orsay*

A deep romantic involvement with the Countess Josephine di Castiglione may account for his long stay in Lviv. She was a singer whom he often accompanied on the piano, and whose children he was hired to instruct

Franz Xaver Mozart was a *musical child prodigy.* At the age of five he gave his first concert in the Vienna Opera and at fourteen he wrote his first piano concerto

Mozart's Requiem for the first time in Lviv — an unprecedented musical event for the city.

From the Choir of St. Cecilia, Franz Xaver created an Institute of Singing, which became the first musical school in Lviv and laid the foundation for the future creation of a conservatory.

Franz Xaver lived in Lviv for almost 30 years. Here he wrote his best compositions, including sonatas, variation cycles, choral cantatas and several piano pieces, based on Ukrainian folk music. Although deeply influenced by the mature Classicism of his father, he also captured, to an extent, the spirit of early Romanticism.

Franz Xaver Mozart returned to Vienna a few years before his death. But the Lviv period remains the most important and most prolific of his life — both for him as a composer, and for the city, where he launched a new era of music.

Aleksander Fredro

Poland's most distinguished playwright Aleksander Fredro (1793–1876) lived in Lviv for almost his entire life. His image is so closely intertwined with the city's image that 19th century Lviv is often referred to as "Fredro's Lviv"

No other writer has been able to capture the spirit, customs and language of 19th century Galicia with as much accuracy, wit and colour as Aleksander Fredro did in his comedies. His main characters are middle class city dwellers and the indigent aristocracy. While he depicted them with great affection, he also sharply satirized their pettiness and conservatism.

Count Fredro was born to a wealthy, noble family on their estate near Lviv. In his youth, he participated in Napoleon's campaigns and recounted those experiences with humour in his memoirs.

He was reputed to be miserly and a misanthrope, even though he took an active part in the city's social life and tried

The memory of Aleksander Fredro survived the Soviet era despite the authorities' effort to get rid of all traces of the bourgeois past. *The street he lived on still bears his name,* but a statue of him on the same street was moved to Poland immediately after World War II. Today, a monument to the Ukrainian historian Mykhailo Hrushevskyi stands in its place

Aleksander Fredro,
Comedies, Volume 5,
Lviv, 1838

Stamp, **Portrait of
Aleksander Fredro,
Poland**, 1980

Left:
Maksymilian
Fajans,
**Portrait of
Aleksander
Fredro**, after
1852

**Actors of
Revenge
Comedy**,
1900

to revamp it in every possible way. For many years, Fredro was a member of the Galician Sejm (the local Parliament). Here he pushed for the establishment of a bank in Lviv, and for a railroad that would connect the city with the capital, Vienna. He had to wait almost 20 years, however, for the railroad to be completed.

Aleksander Fredro lived a long life and died at the age of 83 in Lviv, having earned the title of Honorary Citizen of Lviv.

Fredro's comedies fill the playbills of theatres both in Poland and in Ukraine. In Lviv, you can watch them in the *Polish People's Theatre* operating in the Oblast Teachers' House

Leopold von Sacher-Masoch

The author (1836–1895) — whose name provided a title to a whole concept in psychiatry and sexopathology — lived in Lviv only until he was twelve

When Lviv, Prague, and even Venice shared borders and were all ruled from Vienna by the Habsburg dynasty, people born in these cities became Austrians by default. The Austrian writer Leopold von Sacher-Masoch (born in Lemberg, modern-day Lviv), wasn't spared this fate. Though, according to some sources, his mother was Ukrainian and his father had distant Spanish roots.

Sacher-Masoch's links to the area were short-lived. And yet, Halychyna (the region around Lviv, Ternopil and Ivano-Frankivsk) was a central feature of his literary work. Many of his stories depict everyday life in Halychyna and the seman-

In the 19th century about 15 of Sacher-Masoch's works *were published in Halychyna*

Masoch-Cafe, 7 Serbska St., Lviv

tics of Eastern European sexuality. Many places in Lviv are associated with Sacher-Masoch's persona.

Tourists might be particularly interested in the thematic Masoch-Cafe, which is designed as a museum of eroticism and masochism — a monument to the author graces the entrance. Many of Lviv's theatres keep Sacher-Masoch's memory alive by staging performances based on his works. The famous Grand Hotel in central Lviv replaced the building where von Sacher-Masoch was born.

Wanda von Sacher-Masoch, a long time fan of Sacher-Masoch, *became his wife*

Ivan Franko

Ivan Franko remains one of Ukraine's most important intellectuals of all time, and was considered a walking encyclopedia or polymath

The official complete works of Ivan Franko (1856–1916) comprise 50 volumes. He was a poet, writer, scholar, translator, journalist, social activist and inventor. Franko was born in a village near Lviv. His mother came from an impoverished noble family and his father was a wealthy village artisan-blacksmith.

Franko came to Lviv in 1875 to study philosophy at the Lviv University. As a student he read Karl Marx and Friedrich Engels, and took part in socialist circles. Within five years, the Austrian authorities arrested him twice on charges of "inciting the peasants against the government".

Expelled from Lviv University for his socialist beliefs, he defended his dissertation in Vienna. But he was never able to become a lecturer in Lviv for political reasons. Instead, he worked for Ukrainian newspapers and made his living by publishing articles sporadically. The pay was very low, and for most of his life, Franko lived in poverty.

Though he became disillusioned with leftist ideas later in life, he co-founded several political parties. His invention of a wire-cutting device was helpful to the Ukrainian

Franko had many enemies in the generally conservative Ukrainian environment of Galicia, primarily because of his *leftist views and atheism*

Ivan Franko is buried at the *Lychakivskiy Cemetery* in Lviv. On his grave he is depicted as a stone breaker (kamenyar) in reference to one of his most famous poems

army in World War I, but brought him no profits. He also drafted a law on fishing in Galicia.

The broad scope of Franko's intellect and his incredible productivity help to explain the astounding range of his achievements. In addition to writing lyrical poetry, epic poems, novels, fairy tales and parables, he also translated literary works from 14 different languages into Ukrainian. He wrote research papers on the history of literature, philosophy, linguistics, ethnography, oriental studies, economics, history and psychology.

Through his writing and activism, Franko made a huge impact on the national identity of Galician Ukrainians and their sense of unity with Ukrainians of the Left Bank, which was part of the Russian Empire. At the same time, he was an intellectual of international calibre, maintaining friendly relations with Polish, German, Czech and Russian writers and thinkers.

He passed away from chronic rheumatism. A Memorial Museum, dedicated to him, is currently located at #150 Ivana Franka Street.

18

Ivan Trush

Known as the "painter of the sun", he was one of Ukraine's most outstanding impressionist painters

Ivan Trush (1869–1941) was a Lviv painter and art critic whose favourite genres were landscapes and portraiture.

While studying at the Krakow Academy of Art, he became interested in France's Modernism style of painting and started experimenting with colours and shapes. His use of colour, which was a fresh and new approach for Ukrainian art, became his trademark.

Trush's tranquil and contemplative landscapes are filled with soft light. He was the first artist to depict the Ukrainian Carpathians in an impressionist style. But the setting of his landscapes goes well beyond Ukraine. In seeking the sun and the wealth of its hues, he travelled southwards to Crimea, Italy, Egypt and Palestine.

In 1904 he produced one of his best paintings entitled *Sunset in the*

Trush was so popular that, after his death, *many copies and fakes* made in his unique style appeared in Lviv. During the German occupation, people in Lviv would use Trush's paintings to bribe Nazis, though it was never certain if the paintings were genuine or not

Though Trush *never had any formal students,* nor did he teach anywhere, a whole group of artists in Lviv at the end of the 20th century called themselves his followers. Today, the Lviv Art College bears his name

Ivan Trush produced an astonishing *six thousand paintings*. He considered only a few of them to be real works of art due to his excessive self-criticism

Paintings of Ivan Trush (Clockwise):
Venice, San Giorgio Maggiore island (1908), **In the Garden,**
Sunset in the Forest (1904)

Wood. He tried on several more occasions to replicate the magnetic effect of the bright yellow setting sun, but was unable to achieve the same effect as in his first painting.

Ivan Trush's portraits depict Ukraine's top intelligentsia at the turn of the 19th and the 20th centuries, including writers Lesia Ukrain-ka and Ivan Franko, composer Mykola Lysenko, and historian Mykhailo Hrushevsky.

The street where Trush lived is named in his honour. Also, the Ivan Trush Memorial Museum of Art is located in his former house on #28 Ivan Trush Street.

Solomiya Krushelnytska

Wagnerian diva of the 20ᵗʰ century, world's best opera singer

The most beautiful and charming Madam Butterfly. These and many other enthusiastic and laudatory words are addressed to Ukrainian singer Solomiya Krushelnytska (1872–1952) who conquered the world with her golden soprano.

Solomiya was born into a priest's family in Western Ukraine and showed a propensity for singing from early childhood. When the time came for her to choose a profession, she, with ease, entered the Lviv Conservatory and, after graduation, continued her studies in Italy.

Starting in 1895, this Ukrainian singer triumphantly performed on the stages of the best theatres of the world from Europe to Africa to South America. Her singing was admired by Fyodor Shalyapin and Enrico Caruso, Tito Ruffo and Giacomo Puccini. Solomiya Krushelnytska was the 'prima donna' in many famous opera productions.

In 1920, at the peak of her fame, she left the big stage and traveled Western Ukraine to give chamber performances. When the Soviet authorities took over, Krushelnytska turned to teaching.

The Lviv Opera Theatre is named after her and a memorial museum has been opened in the apartment where she used to live.

Giacomo Puccini was a big fan of Solomiya Krushelnytska. A legend holds that her performance saved his 1904 Milan production of Madame Butterfly

Martin Buber

One of the greatest moral authorities of the 20th century, a philosopher, theologian and theorist of Zionism

Martin Buber (1878–1965) spent his childhood and youth in Lviv. He came from a Lviv Jewish family of religious scholars. His grandfather Solomon was a Talmud expert and researcher, co-chair of the Jewish Congregation and a member of charitable societies.

Martin Buber was born in Vienna. His mother left the family when he was a young boy and then his grandparents took him into their care at their home in Lviv. He graduated from an academic school and took a strong interest in theology and philosophy. He later recalled the day an older child told him, on his grandparents' balcony, that his mother would never come back. He felt this conversation was the first real dialogue in his life, which deeply influenced his future philosophic inquiries into dialogue and the "I-Thou" relationship.

Another significant impact on Buber's future philosophic inquiries was Lviv's linguistic and ethnic diversity. He knew 12 languages, many of which he learned while in Lviv. He was interested in translation

Albert Einstein and Mahatma Gandhi were Martin Buber's close friends and intellectual companions

Buber was *an ecumenist.* Pope John Paul II emphasized his role in the convergence of the world's religions

One of the most famous portraits of Martin Buber was made by *Andy Warhol*, the American pop art creator, as part of his Ten Portraits of the Most Influential Jews of the Twentieth Century series

Book cover, **I and Thou**, by Martin Buber, Touchstone Publishing house, New York, 1971

and the possibility of intercultural dialogue. His translation of the Old Testament into German is considered one of the best.

At the age of 14, Martin Buber moved to his father's house in Vienna. He later studied at universities in Vienna and Berlin, and wrote philosophical essays and articles on Hasidism and Zionism. In the days of Nazi rule, Buber resigned from his professorship at the University of Frankfurt in protest against anti-Semitic policies. In 1934, after harshly criticizing Nazism in a speech in the Berliner Philharmonie, he was banned from speaking in public.

In 1938, Buber and his family moved to Palestine. Still he remained a voice of hope for the persecuted Jews in Europe. Neither the Holocaust nor the Israeli-Egyptian war shook Buber's faith in humanity and the power of interpersonal dialogue.

Buber's last visit to Lviv was in 1935 for his father's funeral. He died in Jerusalem as a world-renowned philosopher.

21

Jan Henryk de Rosen

The life of this Polish artist was full of paradoxes. His career in art began in Lviv, where you can now see some of his outstanding religious murals

As a young man, Jan Henryk de Rosen (1891–1982), the son of a well-known Polish artist of Jewish descent, was mostly interested in military art and diplomacy, not fine art. For a period of time he worked as military advisor to the League of Nations in Geneva.

In the 1920s, de Rosen turned his attention to fine art and had his first exhibitions in Warsaw. There, the religious paintings of the young modernist artist drew the attention of the Armenian Archbishop Jozef Teodorowicz of Lviv. Having just begun the restoration of the ancient Armenian Cathedral in Lviv, the Archbishop offered de Rosen the job of decorating the interior.

This was a major undertaking. The Armenian Cathedral Church on #7 Virmenska Street is one of the most important architectural monuments in the city. It was built in the 14th century following traditional Armenian sacral architecture, and was rebuilt afterwards a number of times. In the beginning of the 20th

*Frescoes of Jan de Rosen in the **Armenian Cathedral**, Lviv*

The Armenian community has existed in Lviv since the beginning of the city's existence, and the *first Armenian Church* was built in Lviv in the 13th century. Today the Armenian community in Lviv is centred on the cathedral that was returned to faithful churchgoers in 2000, after a long period of Soviet neglect. The Armenian Apostle Church Liturgy takes place every Sunday. The local choir is well known for its mesmerizing ancient chants

The Armenian Church is not the only place in Lviv with frescoes by de Rosen. Magnificent wall paintings can also be seen in the Chapel of the Church of the Presentation of the Lord on *#30 Vynnychenka Street*

century, the original interior was restored and an extension was added.

It is in this extension, on the side by Krakivska Street, where you can find the frescoes of Jan Henryk de Rosen. The traditional Eastern patterns of the cathedral harmonize beautifully with de Rosen's Secession wall paintings, which are mysterious and unusual.

One of the frescoes depicts the funeral procession of St. Odilon. The ghostly images of the deceased monks in the procession are quite startling. One in particular stares directly at the viewer, and his features look like those of the artist himself.

In the 1930s, de Rosen lived in Lviv and was a Professor at the Lviv Polytechnic. Prior to World War II he received a proposal to decorate the Polish Embassy in Washington. Due to the outbreak of World War II, he remained in the United States and created dozens of frescoes, mosaics and paintings. He never returned to Europe.

Stanislaw Lem

"Lviv is a part of me and I am a part of Lviv.
I am rooted into this city like a tree," said this
world-renowned Polish fantasy writer

Author of science fiction novels, philosopher and futurologist Stanislaw
Lem (1921–2006) was born in Lviv
and spent the first 25 years of his life
there.

As the son of a wealthy laryngol-
ogist in Lviv, Lem was surrounded in
his formative years by medical par-
aphernalia and scientific books in
his father's library. He later recalled,
"My fate and my calling as a writer
was already budding in me when
I looked at the skeletons, galaxies
in astrophysical tomes, pictures of
reconstructions of the monstrous

extinct saurians of the Mesozoic
era, and coloured human brains in
anatomical handbooks."

In *The High Castle*, a memoir
about his childhood in Lviv, Lem
humorously described himself as
a monster child who gorged himself with sweets and broke his toys
ruthlessly. But his French governess
assured that he learned to read and
write early on, and as a high-school
student he was acknowledged by the
Education Administration to be the
most intelligent child in Southern
Poland.

Stanislaw Lem is *the world's most popular Polish writer.* His books have been translated into 44 languages and have sold over 30 million copies

Having left Lviv at the age of 25, Lem never visited it again, preferring to keep it in his memory as an ideal place

Left: **Stanislaw Lem in 1966**, *courtesy of his secretary, Wojciech Zemek*
Above: **Solaris**, *movie poster, directed by Andrei Tarkovsky in 1972. Covers of Stanislaw Lem's books published by Harcourt Publishing house:* **Solaris** *(1970),* **Fiasco** *(1987),* **Eden** *(1989),* **The Cyberiad** *(1974)*

For Lem, his Lviv period was a time of peace and harmony, great revelations, rambles in the city and ascents to the High Castle, which for him and his friends was "like the heavens for Christians." It was during his time in Lviv that Lem wrote his first poems, published only after World War II.

Lem's graduation from the Gymnasium almost coincided with the Red Army's occupation of Lviv. He was not allowed, by the Soviet regime, to study at the Polytechnic as he wished because of his "bourgeois" origin. Only due to his father's connections was he accepted to the Medical Institute. However,

he purposely did not take his final examinations, so as not to be obliged to become a military doctor in the Soviet Army.

During the Nazi occupation, Lem stayed in Lviv working as a welder in the Wehrmacht's garages while supplying members of the Polish anti-Nazi resistance with ammunition and gunpowder stolen while picking up scrap metal. He risked his life hiding a Jewish friend in the attic of his house.

In 1946, Lem's family was resettled in Poland, away from Soviet-occupied Lviv. He remained in Krakow (aside from a few breaks in the 1980s) until his death.

Batyars

These vagabonds and petty criminals first appeared on the streets of Lviv before World War II. Today their history has gained legendary status

The origin of the word "batyar" is debated, but some say it comes from the Hungarian word "betyar", which means a thief and adventurer.

Batyars were a unique phenomenon of the city's subculture, and were found only in Lviv. This subculture came to life in the mid-19th century in the old artisans' quarter of Lychakiv and in Pohulyanka Park, which used to be a favourite park of Lvivites. Batyars gathered in the Park around the so-called 'small orchards', or pubs.

At first the Batyars were just common thieves. They lived off of pickpocketing, and could sometimes be caught beating and robbing people in the backstreets. They engaged in this kind of petty crime more for the love of adventure than for bounty. Within a couple of decades, batyars stopped stealing and became politically active. Their favourite activity was ridiculing the Austrian Emperor and authorities, while deliberately provoking the police. Their irreverence extended to playing

The Batyars' folklore and parlance were *almost forgotten during Soviet times*, but after 1991, this layer of urban culture slowly came back to life. Some Lviv musicians perform Batyars' songs. Batyar Day takes place almost every year in May, invoking the atmosphere of pre-war Lviv. On these days, you may meet fancily-dressed Batyars all over the city of Lviv. Web-site: batyar.lviv.ua

Viktor Morozov is one of the most famous present-day performers of Batyar songs. We encourage you to check out his records entitled Sertse Batyara ('Batyar's Heart') from 2010, and Batyarskyi Blyuz ('Batyar Blues') from 2013

Left: Yaroslav Pstrak, **Lviv dudes:** **relaxing on a weekend**

practical jokes and flaunting their roguish behaviour. They disliked real criminals and sometimes got into fights with them.

Batyars created a body of specific urban folklore, which included an entire dialect of slang. Because of the diverse population of Lviv at the time, their parlance drew on Polish, Ukrainian, German, Yiddish and their own peculiar Batyar words.

Batyar songs are another aspect of this folklore. Lively and sentimental, these songs have a touch of vulgar humour. At the same time, they poeticize the Batyar 'code of honour', where valour is the main virtue.

24

Sviatyi Sad

In the 1960s and 1970s, Lviv was a legendary mecca for hippies coming from all parts of the Soviet Union

At the end of the 1960s, the neglected garden of the former Carmelites monastery at #22 Vynnychenko Street (now the monastery of the Studite Order and St. Michael Church) became the main gathering place for free-thinking young people. These people listened to rock music, sported long hair, and presented themselves as hippies.

This was the time when the first rumours of a hippie subculture started penetrating the 'iron curtain' of the Soviet Union, and it quickly found its place here. Lviv, as one of the largest European cities of the Soviet Union, 'western' in architecture and in spirit, was attractive to hippies. They came here to hang out, to swap books and music, to play music and to sing together, or just to enjoy the liberating 'bohemian' atmosphere.

In the Soviet Union, *hippies were believed to be dangerous anti-government "elements"* and were subject to persecution. Most hippies did in fact readily provoke and ridicule the government. The very fact that 'the Sacred Garden Republic' actually raged right beneath the windows of the Regional Committee of the Communist Party was considered audacious

Communism is the **youth of the world**

In 1968, the young people who would gather in the garden announced the creation of the informal 'Republic of the Sacred Garden', which even had its own flag and anthem. On the territory of their "Republic", they discussed news pertaining to global rock music and arranged concert sessions. In the summers of 1976 and 1977, two informal festivals were conducted here, with hippies from all corners of the Soviet Union taking part.

Sviatyi Sad became the scene for like-minded people, including school and university students, artists, regular hippies and vagabonds. Even some priests from the underground Ukrainian Greek Catholic Church took part.

Today everything is quiet in the Sacred Garden. It is a cozy green nook in the city centre, and a nice place to stop for a rest when it's hot out.

Many outstanding Lvivites were part of the Sacred Garden group. Among them is Ilko Lemko, writer and Lviv expert. He is the author of many books about Lviv, where he retells Lviv's history through interesting and little-known stories. You can read his book, *The Legends of Old Lviv*, in the English language (Lviv 2010)

25

Dudaryk Choir

The music card of Lviv and Ukraine

It started as the Dudaryk Boys and Men Choir, been knowns as Dudaryk Folk Chapel Choir and State Chapel Choir, only to finally become Dudaryk State Academic Chapel Choir.

Having reached the global recognition and gained undeniable authority, the chapel choir confirms its unique level with every performance, the National Shevchenko Award - the highest Ukrainian state award in culture - and many others are the best proof to that.

Founded in 1971 by acclaimed Ukrainian choirmaster Mykola

In 1985, the chapel choir has founded *the First Choir School in Ukraine*. And have stated their place under the sun and mastered their vocal skills for almost fifty years

Katsal with the support of Ukrainian Music Society in Lviv, Dudaryk has since conquered the leading scenes of the world. The choir had more than 2,500 concerts in the most prestigious Ukrainian and world concert halls, including the Carnegie Hall, Notre-Dame de Paris (the Cathedral of Our Lady of Paris), Air Place Vancouver, the Warsaw Philharmonic, the Ukraine Palace, the National Opera of Ukraine, the National Philharmonic. Dudaryk versatility surprises the audience: their repertoire covers the wide range of ancient and contemporary choral music.

They never interpret the world-known classic masterpieces in a standard way, they create a unique Ukrainian reading, full of the timbre beauty and striking richness of the dynamic palette.

Dudaryk sings with leading orchestras, supervised by the world-class conductors in the best concert halls of the world.

26

Lviv Art Gallery

The largest art museum in Ukraine, this complex's exposition halls are housed in a number of historical landmarks, including the Pidhirtsi Castle

The Lviv National Art Gallery is the most highly regarded of all of Lviv's art museums. Back in the late 19th century, it was decided that a gallery of European art should be established in Lviv. The first paintings that were purchased were by Polish artists, including Jan Matejko. His famous Portrait of the Artist's Children is one of the gallery's trademarks. In 1907, the city magistrate purchased the art collection of Ivan Yakovych (often written Jan Jakowicz), a Ukrainian sugar mag-

nate from Podillya, which included over two thousand pieces of Western European art. This collection became the centrepiece of the gallery.

Today, alongside the Ukrainian and Polish collections, you will find paintings by Italian, Flemish, Dutch, French, Chinese and Japanese artists. Among the most valuable are the works by Peter Paul Rubens, Titian and Hokusai.

The main part of the display is housed in two buildings, in the gallery on #3 Stefanyka Street and

In the courtyard of the Potocki Palace you can stroll through the Park of Castles and Fortifications, another part of the Art Gallery complex. This outdoor exhibition of miniatures displays some of the *ancient defensive structures of Ukraine on a 1:50 scale*. Some of the original structures have been completely destroyed (such as the Lviv High Castle) and only ruins remain from others, such as the Knights Templar Castle in the Zakarpattya region. The models are on display from the middle of March through the middle of October

Left: Jan Matejko, **Portrait of the Artist's Children**. *From left to right: Jerzy (1873–1927), Tadeusz (1865–1911), Helena (Unierzyska, 1867–1932), Beata (Kirchmayer, 1869–1926), 1879*

Right: **Peter Rubens, Portrait of a man**, XVII cent.

Leopold Loeffler, **Portrait of Mariya Savichevska**, 1861

in the magnificent classical Potocki Palace on #15 Kopernyka Street. In the courtyard behind the Potocki Palace, an inconspicuous building houses the Museum of Ancient Ukrainian Books, another branch of the Lviv Art Gallery. Fascinating manuscripts from the 15th century await you there.

The Museum of Sacral Baroque Sculpture by Johann Georg Pinzel, housed in the former Church of Poor Clares on #2 Mytna Square, is also a part of the Lviv Art Gallery complex.

27

The Les Kurbas Theatre

This critically acclaimed theatre has acquired a legendary reputation both here and abroad. Its exploratory interpretations have made it a rich laboratory for all the theatrical arts

In 1988, in the twilight of the Soviet era, a group of young actors, who were dissatisfied with the conservatism of Ukrainian theatre at the time, established this vibrant and innovative theatre. Bristling against the restrictions imposed by socialist culture, the actors created this independent venue for the free expression of the dramatic arts.

The theatre's repertoire is very eclectic, ranging from the dialogues of Plato and texts by the 18th century Ukrainian writer and philosopher Hryhoriy Skovoroda to the classic literature of Shakespeare, Chekhov, Dostoyevskyi and Lesya Ukrainka, and also to such modern dramatists as Ingeborg Bachmann, Eric-Emmanuel Schmitt and Samuel Beckett.

According to founder and director Volodymyr Kuchynskyi, his theatre

The theatre venue is located in a magnificent building on *#3 Les Kurbas Street* which has medieval decorative features. In the first half of the 20th century, it housed a casino, a variety show and a cinema. Unfortunately, we can only appreciate the luxurious crystal chandeliers, gilt detailing and murals that once decorated the theatre hall from pre-war photos on display. However, the theatre corridors still hold the backstage secrets and mysteries of the past

The Les Kurbas theatre initiated several other art projects, with *Word and Voice* Lviv Theatre Center being the most successful. Ancient Ukrainian singing techniques are taught there and are used in acting practice (wordvoice.org). You can learn more at the Les Kurbas Theatre's website: en.kurbas.lviv.ua

combines "eastern meditation" and "western improvisation." The theatre performances are very dynamic and full of music, since all its actors are adept singers and dancers. They also create a special meditative atmosphere inherent to eastern ritual practices.

Spectators are always engaged in the theatre performances. They are often invited to participate in dialogues or even join in the actors' actions. It is symbolic of this engagement that the actors mostly play in the auditorium, while spectators sit on the stage.

Les Kurbas (1887–1937), in whose honour the theatre is named, is the father of modern Ukrainian theatre and one of the most significant Ukrainian theatre directors of the 20th century.

28

Braty Hadiukiny

Braty Hadiukinky were one of Ukraine's most successful bands in Soviet times, and they are still hugely popular today

This band was formed in Lviv in 1988 at a time when, due to Russification policies, not many Ukrainian language bands existed. They mix different genres of music including rock'n'roll, blues, folk, funk and reggae. Fans immediately appreciated the band's songs for their use of irony and both Galician and Russian slang in their colloquial lyrics.

Braty Hadiukiny (Hadiukiny Brothers) had much early success in festivals and concerts both in and outside of Ukraine. However, in 1996 they stopped performing as it became in-

The name "Braty Hadiukiny" means Hadiukin (Viper) Brothers, and comes from a Russian children's story called *The death of Hadiukin the Spy*. It was the group's original leader Oleksandr Yemets who came up with this name

5th album by Braty Hadiukiny
***Made in Ukraine**, 2014*

creasingly difficult to organize concerts and technically support a nine-member band.

After a ten-year break, Braty Hadiukiny held a comeback concert in Kyiv in the winter of 2006. The concert gathered a record number of 15,000 fans, despite the the freezing temperatures (-28°C) outside.

Lead singer Serhiy Kuzminskyi passed away from throat cancer in 2009 and was buried in Lviv's Lychakiv cemeterary.

The band continues to hold concerts and in 2014 it released its first album since 1996.

In the fall of 2014 and 2015, Braty Hadiukiny went on an all-Ukraine tour to promote their new album, *Made in Ukraine*, and *and raise money for the war effort in Eastern Ukraine*

29

Dzyga

At the end of Virmenska Street, you will find the heart of Lviv's contemporary culture, the Dzyga Art Association

In the warmer months, the outside patio of the cafe in front of Dzyga is usually packed with Lviv's artistic elite. It is especially crowded during various music and literary festivals.

Dzyga is actually a contemporary art gallery and a coffeehouse called "Under the Clepsydra (water clock)". But that is not all.

Dzyga was started in 1993 by a group of artists, activists and entrepreneurs who wanted to create a new and independent culture in Lviv. After the creation of the gallery, the group began organizing music and art festivals.

Such festivals as Jazz Bez, the ethno-jazz festival Flyugery Lvova (Weather-Vanes of Lviv), and the Week of Actual Art, one of the biggest contemporary art festivals in Ukraine, are very popular.

The Days of Performance Art and the School of Performance are traditionally held as a part of the Current Art Week. Every year in the beginning of September, *the historical part of Lviv turns into one large stage for several days*

Near the entrance to the Renaissance era building in which the Dzyga gallery is located, there is a monument to the Smile by sculptor Oleh Derhachov, which is the smallest monument in Lviv. *Every seven years*, the existing monument on this spot is replaced with a new one. Also, if you look up to the third floor of the Dzyga gallery building, you will see a staircase leading up into the sky

*Yurko Dyachyshyn, **Slavik's Fashion**, an exhibition at Dzyga Gallery, Lviv, 2015*

Dzyga is a community of people who are united by their openness towards innovative ideas. The three "sub-clubs", (Ethno-club—the club of ethnic music, the Photoclub "5x5", and the JazzClub) meet regularly.

The Dzyga gallery and coffeehouse are located at #35 Virmenska Street.

The performances happen everywhere: on the streets, in the courtyards and in exhibition halls. Artists from Ukraine, Poland, Israel and many other countries participate in the event

30

Okean Elzy

Ukraine's most internationally renowned rock band, OE is also hugely popular at home in Ukraine

The band Okean Elzy (which translates to Elza's Ocean) was formed in 1994 in Lviv. In 1995, the band began participating in high profile concerts and festivals in Ukraine, made its first music video and released its first unofficial single. In 1996, OE took part in a number of festivals abroad.

In 1998, OE released their first album, *Tam, de nas nema* (There, where we are not). Since that time, the band's songs have been heard continuously and everywhere in Ukraine. The band has also gained widespread popularity in Russia, even though the lyrics are sung in Ukrainian. In total, they have released nine albums.

The band's permanent front man Svyatoslav Vakarchuk is a charismatic vocalist who is highly respected by both young and old all throughout Ukraine. As a public activist and philanthropist, he is repeatedly rated as one of the most influential Ukrainians. He also holds a PhD in Physics.

Okean Elzy's lineup has changed several times. *The second permanent member of the band after Vakarchuk is the percussionist, Denys Hlinin.* The band's lineup of 1998–2004 also included guitarist Pavlo Gudimov, bass guitarist Yuriy Khustochka and keyboardist Dmytro Shurov. All of them left the band eventually to develop their own projects, including Gudimov, Esthetic Education and Pianoboy

For their 20th anniversary Okean Elzy performed at the largest stadium in Kyiv in front of *75,000 fans.* This concert holds the record of being the largest solo concert to ever take place in Ukraine

Former members: Denis Hlinin, Pavlo Gudimov, Svyatoslav Vakarchuk, Yurii Khustochka, Dmytro Shurov
Current members: Milos Jelic, Svyatoslav Vakarchuk, Vladimir Opsenica, Denis Dudko, Denis Hlinin

It is Vakarchuk who writes most of the band's lyrics. In addition, Svyatoslav has released two solo projects, the jazz album *Vnochi* (At night) and the jazz-rock album *Brussels*, in cooperation with musicians from Okean Elzy.

Fans and music critics love Okean Elzy for their original melodies, lyricism without excessive sentimentality, unmistakable and inimical vocal style and touching lyrics. Their musical genre might be described as melodic soft rock springing from Britpop.

31

Open Group

Open Group developed out of regular get-togethers between artist friends. Now it is one of the most interesting phenomena in contemporary Ukrainian art

The group of six young artists was formed in 2012, and included Yevhen Samborskyi, Anton Varha, Yuriy Biley, Pavlo Kovach, Stanislav Turina and Oleh Perkovskyi. They create conceptual projects intended to question the fine line between art and non-art and between the creator and the audience. As of 2014, Anton Varga, Yuriy Biley, Pavlo Kovach, and Stanislav Turina have remained as permanent group members.

The group's main goal is to create open art spaces, which are accessible to anyone or any thing. The resulting composition of people and/or things becomes the subject or object of the piece of art. Often the artists of Open Group create an artistic plane that takes on its own life, as in the case of their regular Open Gallery project. This project, the *Gallery on Road #2*, has only start and finish lines, and in between it runs through Ukraine, Moldova, the Black Sea and the Azov Sea areas for more than 1000 km.

In 2013, the Open Group was

The Open Group lives up to its name by having *an open membership policy*. Artists may become members of the group for the duration of joint projects

More and more often, the Open Group represents Ukrainian art abroad. In 2015, they were among the main participants of the *Ukrainian pavilion at the Venice Biennale*

The Detenpyla Gallery has *no fixed timetable*. Anyone who wants to visit it should agree on a time with the artists via e-mail or phone, as provided on the Gallery's website at detenpyla-gallery.tumblr.com

The website of the Open Group is: *open-group.org*

Open Group, multimedia installation **Exclusively for Internal Use**, *2015*

granted the prestigious Pinchuk Art Centre Prize for their Ars Longa, Vita Brevis project. This was a in essence a reality show in which the daily lives of the project's participants were broadcast live to an exhibit space in the Pinchuk gallery.

In 2011, three members of the Open Group opened the Detenpyla Gallery in Lviv. This is probably the city's smallest art gallery, but has an overwhelming concentration of experimental and discovery-oriented works of art. Previously, this small property housed a laundry room, then a blacksmith's workshop and now it's a kitchen-turned exhibition space featuring the works of promising artists from Ukraine and Europe.

32

Agrafka Art Studio

It was thanks to Agrafka's founders that contemporary Ukrainian book design received exposure abroad and won international acclaim

Andriy Lesiv and Romana Romanyshyn, who created and developed the book brand Agrafka, are united by several factors: they both studied at the Lviv Art College and then at the Lviv National Art Academy, they are married to each other, and they are both artists who adore books.

Romana began her art career as a glass painter and Andriy as an art restorer. While still in college, they received a request to design a book cover, almost by accident. Initially it was a side project, but gradually, book design became a life-long creative passion.

In 2010 they decided to create their first art book, *Rukavychka* (The Mitten), based on the well-known Ukrainian folk tale. A unique part of the book was that it was designed to fit inside a felt casing. After failing to find a publisher, the artists took the bold step of self-publishing it. To their surprise, it became a great success, and soon the pair were contacted by a publishing company offering their services.

Various book covers of **The War that Changed Rondo** *by Romana Romanyshyn and Andriy Lesiv. Ukrainian, Korean, French, and Polish editions*

Agrafka's artists usually combine a variety of techniques including *collage, and only rarely use solely digital technology*. They usually create an image using 'live' material, which they digitally process afterwards. Their style is quite recognizable, and each project is special and unique

The books created or designed by Agrafka have been included in *White Ravens, the world catalogue of the best publications for children,* for several years now

Since then, the Agrafka workshop has created more than 30 books for children and adults, including several art books. Their most successful projects have been those in which everything from the concept to the text and design, have been created by Lesiv and Romanyshyn themselves. Examples include *Stars and Poppy Seeds*, and *The War That Changed Rondo*. Both books received the Bologna Ragazzi Award, the most prestigious children's book award.

The War That Changed Rondo is an attempt to explain the notion of war to children. The idea came to the artists following the start of the conflict in Eastern Ukraine, but its themes are universal. The book has been translated into French, Slovak and Korean.

Agrafka's website: agrafkastudio.com

33

Publishers' Forum

Lviv is often called the "book capital" of Ukraine because of the yearly Publishers' Forum held there

Every year in September, Lviv is transformed by an exciting event called the Publishers' Forum. It started back in 1994, a time of deep economic recession and high inflation, with the idea of bringing together people who write, publish and read books. The first Publishers' Forum offered 25 events in its program, and by 2015 this number had ballooned to 1,440 events.

Thousands of book lovers flock to the city from all over Ukraine and abroad. You can virtually smell fresh printing ink in the air as numerous publishing houses prepare their nov-

elties for the fair. You will notice informal work meetings in full swing in Lviv's coffee houses, as practically all of Ukraine's authors and publishers turn up in Lviv for this event.

The Publishers' Forum has expanded in more than size over the years. It now includes the Publishers' Forum for Children, the Translation Festival, the Art Management and Literary Criticism Festival, and also a young poets contest, modern drama readings and a special program for the elderly.

Of all the events, the International Literary Festival is the most pop-

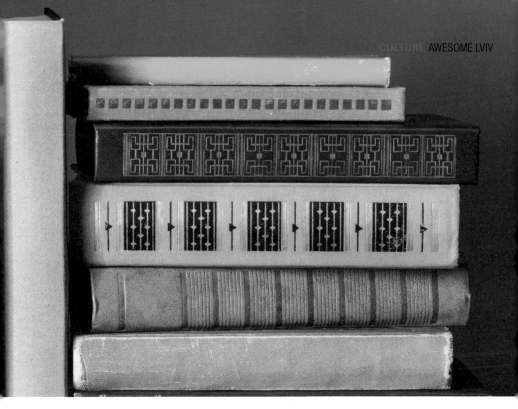

The Potocki Palace (on #15 Kopernyka Street) is one of the forum's main venues. One of the most elegant buildings in Lviv, it is a fine example of French Classicism and was erected in the late 19th century. Today the Potocki Palace is a museum belonging to the Lviv Art Gallery. Next to the Potocki Palace stands the Lviv Art Palace, built in 1996, which hosts art exhibitions throughout the year, and is *the main venue of the Publishers' Forum*

Over the years, the Literary Festival has welcomed such world famous writers as *Erlend Loe, Jostein Gaarder, Paulo Coelho, DBC Pierre, Vladimir Sorokin, Lyudmyla Petrushevska* and hundreds of others

ular. It has been held since 2006 and is one of the biggest literary events in Eastern Europe. Presentations, poetry readings, author meetings, and concerts take place in the dozens of halls, coffee shops and clubs, or sometimes just out in the open. The events start at 10–11 in the morning and continue until late at night. A delightful tradition is the Night of Poetry and Music, which brings together hundreds of spectators. All night long you can listen to the poets' performances accompanied by rock, folk and jazz music stars.

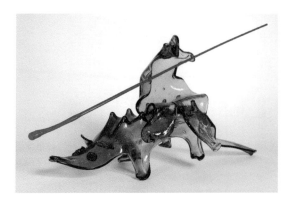

34

Bokotei Glass

Lviv huta glasswork is a unique phenomenon in Ukrainian art

Artistic glassware had been produced in Halychyna since 11the century, and by the end of the 20th century, the city of Lviv could boast of more than 20 enterprises that manufactured different kind of glass — construction, technical, artistic, etc.

It was in Lviv where, based on the venue of Lviv Experimental Ceramic and Sculpture Factory, thousands of samples of vases, utensils and glass souvenirs were produced, and a special brigade of huta glassblowers was created to work directly with the glass painters. Artist from all over the former Soviet republics came here to fulfil their creative ideas for decades.

Lviv has become an artistic base for numerous artists that are now creating the image of Ukrainian glasswork and promote it in the world: Andryi Bokotei, Franz Cherniak, Oles Zvir, Andryi Petrovskyi, Ihor Matsiyevskyi to name a few.

Since 1962, *the Lviv National Art Academy has a unique department of art glass, only one in Ukraine.* The students master different techniques of artistic processing of the glass, and first of all the art of huta glass blowing and forming. They can always rely on the hot-glass furnace, a device that not all of the European universities can boast of having

It was Andryi Bokotei, the leading figure of Ukrainian glass art and one of the first followers of the international studio glass movement, who initiated the International Huta Glass Symposiums in Lviv.

Since 1989, every three years acclaimed glass artists from all over the world come to Lviv to work together by the hot-glass furnace and later to present their pieces at a large-scale exhibition. All of the works created by the international artists during the Symposiums (we've already had 10 of those!) were gifted to Lviv Glass Museum. Thus today the Museum has more than 350 unique exhibits by 250 artists from 32 countries of the world. You can see some of the collection treasures in the very centre of the city: the Glass Museum is situated at the Rynok Square.

35

Alfa Jazz Fest

If you enjoy listening to world-class jazz, come and take in some performances at the Alfa Jazz Fest, one of the major jazz festivals in Europe

The Alfa Jazz Fest has been held each June in Lviv since 2011. The festival takes place on several stages, the main one located in the "Park Kultury". This large stage is where the most prominent jazz stars have their concerts, but anyone who is not able to buy a ticket can watch a direct broadcast from the park lawns. Crowds of people enjoy getting together there for a jazz picnic on the grass.

World-renowned jazz musicians have delighted audiences at the Lviv festival, including Bobby McFerrin, Herbie Hancock, George Benson, Al Di Meola, John McLaughlin, Wayne Shorter, Charlie Haden, Larry Carlton, Charles Lloyd, Cassandra Wilson, Dee Dee Bridgewater, Mike Stern, Hiromi, Avishai Cohen, Eliane Elias and many others.

Smaller festival stages are located on Rynok Square and in the courtyard of the Potocki Palace. Less famous but no less talented young musicians from different countries, and especially from Ukraine, are invited to play there. The entrance to these concerts is free.

The Alfa Jazz Fest may be the only Ukrainian music event broadcast by

Clockwise:
Arturo Sandoval, 2016
Esperanza Spalding, 2016
Dianne Reeves, 2016
Bobby McFerrin, 2013

The park's website:
centralpark.lviv.ua

A special award,
the Alfa Jazz Fest
Award, dedicated
to *Eddie Rosner*,
is presented each
year to one of the
major participants
for distinguished
achievements in
music

Alfa Jazz Fest
may be the only
Ukrainian music
event broadcast
by the European
music channel
Mezzo, and this
undoubtedly
demonstrates the
*high level and
international
significance
of the event.*
The Jazz Times
includes Alfa Jazz
Fest in its list of
major jazz events
in Europe

*The 26-hectare
park*, officially
called the Bohdan
Khmelnytskyi
Park Kultury, had
become somewhat
dilapidated during
the Soviet era, but
has been brought
back to life. It now
hosts many events
besides the jazz
festival, including
fairs, festivals,
concerts, outdoor
movies and sports
competitions

the European music channel Mezzo,
and this undoubtedly demonstrates
the high level and international significance of the event. *The Jazz Times*
includes Alfa Jazz Fest in its list of
major jazz events in Europe.

The festival's website is www.
alfajazzfest.com

36

The Lviv Film Center

At this cinematography and film education centre, you can watch alternative movies in a retro setting

In 2015, a group of cinema enthusiasts decided to refurbish an old Soviet-era cinema and turn it into an interesting venue for film lovers. It now shows numerous high-quality independent or 'uncommon' films and hosts other cultural and educational events as well.

The Lviv Film Center is located in the old Sokil theatre for children, built in 1978 during the last decade of Soviet rule. It is located away from the city centre in the Horikhovyi Hai ('Walnut Grove') Park. A typical 'district' theatre, it is one of many small theatres built at the time in the USSR. The interior style of that era has been preserved. It is comprised

Lviv hosts a few of its own film festivals, including Wiz-Art, the International Short Motion Picture Festival, (*wiz-art.ua/festival*), and the Independent Open Air Movie Festival KinoLew

of concrete and glass, a futuristic ceiling made of panels with geometrical patterns, and optimistic images in stained glass across a large wall.

The movie selection is broad and eclectic, including world and Ukrainian cinema classics, the winners of the largest film festivals, works by representatives of 'small cultures,' and children's movies. For special weekly retro sessions, old film reels are borrowed from the city's archives. From time to time they also hold cinema nights where films can be watched one after the other. You can also see movies from both Ukrainian and international cinema festivals, such as the Kyiv Festival of Documentaries or the Manhattan Short Film Festival. They even show premiers of movies made by young Ukrainian directors.

Many movies are shown in the original languages with Ukrainian subtitles. If you want to watch a movie in Lviv in a friendly and relaxed atmosphere, this is the place for you.

Address: 14a Volodymyra Velykoho street.

Webpage: facebook.com/lviv-filmcenter

FOOD

37

Galician Borshch

Delicious, deep red borshch is one of the most popular dishes of Ukraine

Any vegetable soup with beets as the main ingredient can be considered borshch. Other ingredients vary by personal taste and tradition. Borshch can be made with or without meat, mushrooms, cabbage, beans or even eggs and it may be served hot or cold. Borshch can actually be made even without beets, in which case the base vegetable is the leafy green sorrel, and it is referred to as 'green borscht'.

An important feature of any borshch is a distinct sour note, and Galicians know this very well. This is why Galician borshch is made with a base of strong beet brew, created by fermenting fresh table beets in water.

A true Galician borsch is cooked without meat, and don't believe it, if you are told otherwise. As a rule, mushrooms are used, and oftentimes a pinch of flour cooked with butter (known as "zaprazhka") is added for flavour.

A special component of Galician borsch is 'vushka,' or 'ears'. 'Ears' are envelopes of thin dough containing a filling of mushrooms and fried onions, similar to small varenyky or dumplings. The 'ears' are cooked separately, placed in a bowl, and hot borsch is then poured over them.

Borsch 'with ears' should be served on *Christmas Eve*. Since it's meatless, it is perfect for the last supper of the pre-Christmas Lent, during which 12 dishes are served

38

Syrnyk

Natives of Lviv adore their desserts. It's hard to say which one is Lviv's trademark dessert, but many would likely say it's syrnyk

You can sample syrnyk in virtually every cafe or hostel in Lviv. Syrnyk is a cake somewhat similar to cheesecake that is made from cottage cheese.

Syrnyk is made of sieved high-fat cottage cheese, eggs, sugar and butter. Vanilla, raisins, lemon peel and sometimes candied fruit or other flavourings are added before baking it in the oven. Traditional Lviv syrnyk has a chocolate glaze poured over the top. But of course, every cook has his or her own recipe and special secrets.

Lviv families bake many different kinds of cakes that are referred to as "plyatsky" locally. They mostly consist of several layers with cream and fruit or jam in between the layers, or perhaps cocoa and walnuts. There are plenty of recipes.

During holidays, Lvivites bake several kinds of plyatsky at once. But few people deny themselves sweet treats on regular

When in Lviv, it is also worth trying strudel, pronounced "shtroodel", as in German. A classic strudel is made with apple filling; however, other types of strudel may include, cherries or poppy seeds. Savory strudels with vegetables, cottage cheese and other fillings are made as well. *This dessert came to Lviv from Austria* and flourished in the local cuisine as if it had always been there

days as well, so it is no surprise that there are so many dining outlets in Lviv offering a great selection of first-rate home-baked treats.

Another popular dessert is "tsvibak", a kind of sponge cake in different variations. "Tsvibak" may refer to the basic dough itself, or a sandwiched sponge cake, a plain sponge cake or a sponge cake with candied fruit and nuts.

Lvivites make many different dishes from cottage cheese, both sweet and savoury. Smaller relatives of the great syrnyk are little cheese pancakes with a very similar name, "syrnyky". They are fried and *usually served at breakfast with jam*

39

Halka Coffee

One of the most popular stereotypes
about Lviv is that it is a coffee city

Lviv coffee is wrapped in legends and myths. The facts are as follows: coffee came to Lviv with the transition of the city under the jurisdiction of the Austro-Hungarian Empire, where the coffee-making culture was very well-developed. The first known coffee institution is the Levakovskyi Coffee House, which dates back to 1802. The second is the Vienna Coffee House that was built in 1829, and still operates today on #12, Prospekt Svobody.

The Halka Coffee Factory was the first industrial coffee manufacturing plant launched in Lviv. It started in 1932 as the cooperative factory 'Suspilnyi Promysl' that manufactured 'coffee for the poor', made of chickory and malt substitutes.

During Soviet times, the Lviv Coffee factory manufactured instant coffee that was considered a commodity in short supply at the time. Later on, the production of whole-bean coffee and ground coffee began. Before the Lviv tourism boom launched, Lviv visitors would purchase freshly ground coffee bought at 'Halka' outlets.

Nowadays, coffee from Lviv is not just a brand. Nearly 90% of all Ukrainian coffee is produced by Lviv manufacturers, and more than half of it is made by 'Halka'. You may visit Halka's main shop and cafe at #6 Kovzhuna Street.

A key figure of Lviv coffee legends is *Yuriy Kulchytskyi*. He did actually exist, and was a kozak from the Lviv area. He was rewarded for distinguished service during the Battle of Vienna in 1683. As a reward, he chose 300 bags of Turkish coffee beans, which were not well-known in Europe at the time. He is believed to have developed a coffee culture in Vienna, starting the new fashion of drinking it with sugar and milk. The 'Halka' coffee factory erected a monument to Kulchytskyi in Lviv

Many Lviv cafes and shops sell fresh roasted coffee beans. Coffee connoisseurs and experts recognize "Svit Kavy" on *#6 Katedralna Square* as the oldest, and perhaps the coziest of them all

40

Svitoch Chocolate

Lviv cherishes its well-established reputation as a city of chocolate, caramel and all kinds of sweets. But the history behind this reputation is less well known

In 1882, the first confectionery plant "Branka" was founded in Lviv. Two decades later, the "Gazet" factory appeared. Together they manufactured five thousand tonnes of sweets per annum and there were a few other smaller manufacturers as well. Visiting numerous sweet shops with creatively decorated front windows became a favourite pastime in Lviv.

In Soviet times, the confectioneries "Branka" and "Gazet" formed the basis for the large "Svitoch" factory, established in 1962. Svitoch operated under special conditions; experi-

ments in recipes going beyond the standardized Soviet manufacturing framework were allowed here and the employees found this stimulating. Hence, the products they manufactured were also special.

Chocolatiers from all over the Soviet Union came to study and adopt Svitoch's practices, and people from all over Ukraine sought Svitoch chocolate and candies as the best gourmet sweets. Svitoch products were exported in bulk and Lviv was the chocolate capital of the USSR.

Today, Svitoch is owned by the

Nowadays, *Lviv has made chocolate into a religion almost,* with a chocolate festival held annually in the city. Chocolate and sweet shops are hugely popular, particularly those that make them right in front of you. Some shops specialize in chocolate making, while others focus on lolly pops or marzipan

international food giant Nestlé and does not stand out so much anymore among the numerous competitors in the market. However, some types of Svitoch chocolates, the recipes of which have not changed for decades, remain the favourite goodies of Lvi-vites and of others too.

We recommend trying Stozhary, Romashka and Zoryane Syaivo chocolates, as well as the nostalgic Artek wafers. You can buy them in any shopping centre.

41

Staryi Rynok Liqueur

This is an alcoholic beverage that you won't be able to buy anywhere outside of Lviv, unless you are very lucky! But in Lviv you will find it in every backstreet bar or liquor store

Staryi Rynok (Old Market), which is named after a square of the same name, is a traditional Lviv drink. It is a brandy-based liqueur flavoured with walnut, nutmeg, honey, cinnamon and cardamom. It has an alcohol content of 45%, but because of its sweet taste it's highly drinkable.

In addition to this traditionally flavoured liqueur, there are other varieties such as cherry, chocolate, coffee and lemon. These have a lower alcohol content (25-30 %) than the classic liqueur. Old Rynok is produced by the Lviv spirits factory, which traces its history back to 1931.

Old Rynok can be consumed straight or it can be added to cocktails. For example, the chocolate liqueur is recommended for use in White Russian cocktails, or it can simply be mixed with milk in a ratio of 1:1. All types of Old Rynok can be added to coffee or ice cream.

To be honest, this liqueur is not considered particularly exquisite, perhaps because it has been on the menu of cheap joints since Soviet times. It is rarely served in expensive restaurants. But tastes differ. Many people like it, so you might as well try it and see for yourself.

A bottle of Staryi Rynok is an *excellent local souvenir* from Lviv

Quite a few restaurants in Lviv offer *their own liqueurs and nastoyankas (infusions)*, as a post-meal digestif. So, try a few and find your personal preference!

Lviv was famous for its liqueurs and spirits in the 19th and early 20th century, when the Baczewski spirits factory operated here. The factory used the most advanced technologies and was exceptionally good at marketing.

They exported their products throughout Europe and were granted the title of *Purveyor to the Imperial and Royal Court* of Austro-Hungary. In the 1930s, they even shipped their products by plane

42

Svit Kavy

Svit Kavy (The World of Coffee) is a coffee
shop you should visit for a delicious
morning coffee

Svit Kavy started its story in February 2000 when a coffee shop
was opened at the Katedralna Square, by that time boasting
only tree tables and fresh-made coffee. Today, Svit Kavy is a
three-storied coffee shop and cafe at Katedralna Square to taste
and buy the best coffee, a roastery at Kulparkivska Str, and
roastery-cafe at 30 Rynok Square.

Svit Kavy is an
*ideal place for
the business
meetings*. And
you can also meet
the mayor or
other Ukrainian
celebrities

Its founder Markian Bedriy travels to Central American and African coffee plantations every year, to meet the farmers and choose the green beans of the best quality. Later in Ukraine, the samples are dripped again and only then the final decision whether the beans will be used is made. The coffee varies from season to season, every year the beans origin country is different: at some point, there might be a lot of coffee from Honduras or Ethiopia, and the next year will be all about El Salvador.

You might also be lucky to treat yourself with freshly baked pastry at Katedralna Square, they bake strudels and charlottes at the third floor. In the cafes in the city centre, any of the milk drinks can be made on almond, coconut or lactose-free milk on demand. The self-service system is practised in all of the venues, except for the second and third floors at Katedralna.

Svit Kavy is also a good example of *a family business in Ukraine*: Markian's daughter, Oksana is an administrator at the cafe at Rynok Square, his son Ostap roast the coffee there and his wife Olia is responsible for the new recipes

43

Lviv Beer

While coffee is considered the most popular drink in Lviv, beer, without a doubt, is a close second

One of the most popular types of local beer is *Lviv 1715*. This was the year when Jesuit monks founded the brewery in what was a suburb of Lviv at the time. It is one of the two oldest breweries in Ukraine, and has operated non-stop since the day it was opened.

But beer in Lviv was brewed even before 1715. Back in the 15th century, a brewery shop was opened in Lviv. However, after a hundred years the authorities became concerned, not because of the large amounts of beer brewed, but by its low quality. It came as no surprise that the right to establish an industrial brewery was granted to the monks. Their beer tasted better than that of the local brewers'.

In the days of Austro-Hungarian rule, the Jesuits were deprived of many rights and estates. Their brewery was passed

There is a museum of beer brewing at the Lviv Brewing Factory, which houses a large exhibit on the history of the art of the brewery, and a beer tasting hall

Lviv brewery commercial, 1930s

One "beer tour" begins at Kumpel brewery restaurant on *#6 Vynnychenko Street*

For a certain period of time at the end of the 19th century, German businessman Robert Doms owned the Lviv brewery. He was one of the *most famous benefactors in the history of the city*, and was the founder of a safe haven for artists and writers. The place gave shelter not only to the impoverished artists that needed care, but also to bankrupt merchants and industrialists. His name was given to the Lviv brewery beer restaurant Robert Doms Khmilnyi Dim at #18 Kleparkivska Street, and to one of Lviv's beers, called Old Doms

into private ownership, and became one of the most powerful companies of the Empire. Lviv beer became famous all over Austria-Hungary, particularly because it was suitable for being transported great distances. In the years before additives were introduced, this could only be achieved by strict compliance with technological requirements.

Today there are many more places in Lviv where *craft beer* is produced. In fact, a few companies offer Lviv beer tours

During the times of the Soviet planned economy, the range of beer available was narrowed down to two basic varieties, although they were both considered among the best in the country.

Nowadays, beer brewing has experienced a revival. New varieties pop up regularly and there is even a special Lviv Christmas beer, produced each year for the winter holidays. Lovers of dark beer would enjoy Lviv Porter. In the summertime, the light taste of Lviv Weissbeer is quite refreshing.

44

Virmenka Cafe

Virmenka is a legendary cafe that has remained virtually unchanged since its opening in 1979; the decor and even their method of making coffee are still remarkably the same

The name of the cafe was informal at first but then became official, and derives from its location at #19 Virmenska street. Almost immediately, Virmenka became the scene for liberal youth and artists, musicians, painters and poets. The tiny cafe had limited seating and permitted coffee to be enjoyed outside, a special kind of freedom at a time when cafes didn't have outdoor terraces.

The cafe's patrons enjoyed a freedom in their conversations which was generally considered taboo elsewhere, discussing creative and civil freedoms, non-communist art, underground music and so on.

In addition to traditional Galician desserts such as syrnyk, here you may try a *Turkish delicacy like baklava*. By the way, if you like your coffee with no sugar, make that clear to the barista. Otherwise, sugar is added automatically

Coffee from Virmenka is said to be *the tastiest in town*. It is one of the few cafes in Lviv where coffee is still prepared using the recipe that was very popular in Soviet times. It is made in a cezva, a Turkish-type coffee pot, on a bed of hot sand that is warmed on a special electric stove. The beans are very finely ground and, as a result, the coffee dregs are thick like tar

Not surprisingly, the KGB became interested in this cafe and its patrons. After a local newspaper slammed the 'overly liberal' lifestyle of Virmenka's regulars in a 1982 article, the KGB tried to close it down. Nevertheless, it continued to operate.

Today, Virmenka Cafe is as popular as ever. If you are lucky, you may meet its life-long regulars here and catch the feeling of being carried back decades in time.

PLACES

*Mascaron at the **Segal House***

45

St. Nicholas's Church

Only a few buildings dating back to the very beginning of Lviv's history have survived to this day due to fires, battles, and architectural modernization. One of them is St. Nicolas's Church

The first record of St. Nicholas's Orthodox Church was found in a document from 1292, in which Prince Lev granted the church land ownership of the site. It is most likely the date when the church's construction was completed. Its current address is #26 Khmelnytskyi St., which is the former junction of old trade routes. Fittingly, it was named after St. Nicholas, the patron saint of merchants.

The church was constructed from coarse white limestone, and in accordance with the old Ukrainian architectural tradition it was built in

Today, the *Church of St. John* the Baptist houses the Lviv Museum of Old Monuments, dedicated to the ancient Rus' period of the city's history

Another church located in Lviv's city centre is the Church of Our Lady of Perpetual Help on #2 Snizhna St., formerly known as the *Church of Maria Snizhna or Mary of Snow*. Initially, it was the main church for Lviv's German community. It was most likely a wooden church in the 13th century, reconstructed in stone later on

the shape of a cross and topped with round cupolas. After several reconstructions, the church as it stands today is largely a product of its 17th century reconstruction. Several valuable icons have also survived from that time. The frescoes that adorn the church's facade were added by the Ukrainian statesman and artist Petro Kholodnyi in 1924.

The Church of St. John the Baptist, located on #1 Old Rynok Square, competes with the Church of St. Nicholas for the rank of the oldest existing church in Lviv. It was most likely constructed in 1270. It is a small church with modest décor, built by Prince Lev for his wife Constance.

46

Old Rynok

This is the best starting point for quietly exploring Lviv's many nooks and crannies, just a stone's throw away from the tourist-filled new Ploshcha Rynok (Market Square)

The Old Rynok Square is where the city of Lviv had its origins. Nearby, the remains of a settlement dating back to the 4–5th century AD were found. In the 13th century, the Old Rynok Square became the foundation for the city of Lviv, with its trades and handicrafts on offer not far from the High Castle. It was here that medieval trade routes crossed, leading from the Baltics in the north to Crimea in the south, and from the Tatar east to the European west. International trade bustled at Lviv's Old Rynok Square. The city developed quickly thanks to a law stating that any arriving merchants were required to stay for a few days and sell some of their goods.

In the second half of the 14th century, the construction of a fortified city around the new Rynok Square started. The Old Rynok found itself behind the city walls, in the so-called Zhovkivskyi suburb, where

Left: **Ruins on the territory of the reform synagogue** *at Staryi Rynok Square. Photograph of first post-war years*

In the area around the Old Rynok, you can find some amazing yet strange spots. For example, there is one courtyard with kitschy paintings, old propaganda boards, busts of Soviet-era personas and other junk from Soviet times, carefully collected by somebody, probably, after it had been thrown out by its original owner. There is another yard with a collection of old toys. And if you turn the corner of some of the very normal looking streets, you might come across a pet goat grazing on a lawn. It certainly does make for a unique place. *So drop by and have a look around!*

mainly Jews and some Ukrainians lived.

In 1846, the Temple synagogue was built on Old Rynok Square, which was a monumental classical-style building with a dome. In 1941, the Nazis blew it up along with three other nearby synagogues and moved the neighbourhood's Jewish population to the ghetto. Only one synagogue, a block away from Old Rynok on #3 Vuhilna St., has survived to this day.

Today, there is a small square with an ancient well on the site of the demolished synagogue. The streets around the square are quiet and somewhat neglected. Some of them turn into paths and get lost on the slopes of the High Castle. When more than a century old multilingual inscriptions are exposed from under the plaster, you may get a feeling that Lviv's history is speaking to you from the walls of its stone buildings.

47

The Ratusha

Along with the rest of Lviv, the town hall was built, changed, ruined and reconstructed; but it has always remained the centre of public life and self-governance

The first Ratusha (Town Hall) in Lviv was most likely made of wood. After the fire of 1381, a new, stone, Gothic style town hall replaced the wooden one. In 1404, a clock was put on its tower. At that time, the first floor of the Ratusha was used by tradesmen and the second floor was used by the local council and judges. The basement rooms of the town hall were used as storage rooms, prisons and pubs. The Ratusha repeatedly suffered from fires, but was always restored, rebuilt or expanded in line with new needs.

From the late 18th century, Austrian officers rebuilt the Ratusha in every possible way and demolished many buildings on Rynok Square; however, they always made efforts to preserve the beautiful tower. In 1826, a crack appeared in the tower, but a committee of experts concluded that it didn't pose any danger to the structure. But just as the committee was signing their protocol, the tower collapsed. Most people managed to escape the building, but eight people were buried alive under the rubble.

You can walk up the many steps to get to the Ratusha's tower where you will have an *incredible bird's eye view of the city* from the observation deck. You will also have a good view of Lviv's main clock, installed in 1851

The next town hall was a monumental building which had a tower with a cupola. But this Ratusha was also burned down in 1848. Three years later, it was rebuilt into the Ratusha we can see today, with a massive four-sided tower and with a "medieval" parapet. The citizens of Lviv were extremely unhappy with the design, but today it is hard to imagine the city's panorama without the Ratusha's familiar silhouette.

48

Staroyevreiska Street

One of Lviv's oldest streets, Staroyevreiska has now become one of the most popular areas for an evening out in central Lviv

This quaint pedestrian street has existed since the 13th century. Its buildings, however, are newer, with some dating back to the 17th century Renaissance period, such as #24, 26, and 34. Just as with the bulk of the Rynok Square area, most of the buildings on this street were constructed in the 18th and the 19th centuries, and are decorated with baroque elements.

Staroyevreiska translates to "Old Jewish" street and most of its buildings belonged to the Jewish quarter from medieval times. Lviv's most famous and mythical synagogue "The Golden Rose", once stood between #37 Staroyevreiska and #3 Arsenalska streets. Currently all that remains of the synagogue are its outlines, left on the wall of the adjacent building. Located just across the street was the Great Synagogue, built in the 14th century, and rebuilt many times since. Both temples were

Between buildings 40 and 46 on Staroyevreiska Street you will find the Koliyivshchyna Square, with its small park and old well. It is considered the smallest square in Ukraine. Another of Lviv's squares, Vicheva Square, was also a contender for this title

"Tsukernia", possibly Lviv's most famous cake and pastry cafe, is located on #3 Staroyevreiska Street. Its *cakes are made according to time-honoured Galician and Austro-Hungarian recipes.* A fitting atmosphere of nostalgia and comfort reigns within its walls

Ruins of synagogue *on Staroyevreiska street in Lviv*

demolished during the Nazi occupation

The end of this street joins with the City Arsenal, located at #5 Pidvalna Street. This 16th century fortification used to be a part of the City Wall. Now it is the "Arsenal", a museum of weapons. The popular nightclub 'Under the Arsenal' is located on the ground floor.

49

St George's Cathedral

This beautiful Rococo-styled cathedral is one of the most recognizable buildings in Lviv

This church is well known not only due to its beauty, but also because it can be seen from various spots in Lviv. The hill upon which it stands is one of the highest spots in the city.

St. George's Cathedral has served to this day as the mother church of all Ukrainian Greek Catholic churches. It was originally built of wood in the 13th century by Prince Lev Danylovych upon the advice of his uncle, Prince Vasylko. Prince Vasylko took his monastic vows in old age in order to live a reclusive life in one of the caves here, to redeem himself of his many sins.

The first stone church was built here at the end of the 14th and beginning of the 15th century. At that time it was still a suburb of the city. Due to its position on the hill, the cathedral and adjacent monastery, surrounded by defensive walls, also functioned as a fortress. Lvivites found shelter here during the siege of Lviv by Bogdan Khmelnytskyi's army of kozaks in 1648, and during the Turkish Siege of 1672.

The Cathedral as we know it was built at the end of the 18th century. Its rich décor includes three figures above the portal, which are the most prominent. On the sides above the entryway are two figures representing the fathers of Eastern churches, St. Athanasius and St. Lev (Leo). Interestingly, the church's construction was undertaken by their name-

For many centuries, one of *the largest markets in Galicia* was held every spring at the square near St George's Cathedral. You could buy anything there. Popular traditional sweets on sale were decorated honey and gingerbread cookies in the form of soldiers, baskets, or hearts. They were nicknamed 'Yurshky' to honour St. Yuriy (George) the Patron Saint of the cathedral and the hill. Today the gingerbread shop Yurashky on #14 Krakivska Street reminds us of this Galician tradition

One of the bells on the St. George's Cathedral bell tower is the oldest of its kind in Ukraine. According to the inscription, this bell was cast in 1341

sakes Athanaius Sheptytskyi and Lev Sheptytskyi. Atop the church's main entrance stands a sculpture of the majestic St. George the Dragon-slayer on a horse. All of the sculptures were created by Galician architect Johann Georg Pinsel (Jan Jerzy Pinzel).

The metropolitan chambers were built at approximately the same time as the cathedral. For a long time they served as the residence of the heads of the Ukrainian Greek Catholic Church, but this residence has now been relocated to Kyiv.

The Metropolitan Gardens, or St. George's Park, was designed according to the tradition of Baroque parks, with beautiful retaining walls slightly reminiscent of the Roman viaducts. In 2005, the Metropolitan Gardens were opened to the public. However, the park is currently in a slightly neglected state.

50

The Jesuit Church

The largest cathedral in Lviv, this early Baroque architectural marvel has recently been reopened to the general public

The construction of this cathedral took almost 20 years, from 1610 to 1630. Italian-born architect Jacopo Briano modeled it after the Cathedral of the Holy Name of Jesus (Il Gesu) in Rome and built it from Michelangelo's sketches. This cathedral was a model for Jesuit churches built all across Europe at the time.

One of the most valuable elements of the church's interior is the baroque-styled crucifix on the side altar, created by German-schooled renowned sculptor Johann Pfister, a long-time resident of Lviv.

Attached to the cathedral and the Jesuit monastery was a Collegium School. In 1661, John (Jan) II Casimir, King of Poland, granted this Collegium "the honour of an Academy and the title of University". Thus, the Jesuit Collegium became the first higher education institution in Lviv. It is considered the direct predecessor of the Lviv Ivan Franko National University.

During Soviet times, atheists used most churches, including the Jesuit Cathedral, for various secular purposes, such as *gymnasiums or clubhouses*. For example, the Church of Saint Clement the Pope on #70 Chuprynky St. was used as a telephone station, and St. Anna's Cathedral on #32 Horodotska St. was used as a furniture shop

The highest tower in the town once stood next to the Jesuit Cathedral. It was torn down in 1830, several years after the collapse of the Town Hall's tower, to prevent another disaster

Among the most famous graduates of the College was Bohdan Khmelnytskyi, the future Hetman of the Zaporizhian Host. Though a national hero, his role in Lviv's history is quite controversial. In 1648, during the war between the Ukrainian Kozaks and Rzceczpospolita Polska (Poland), his troops besieged Lviv, a Polish city at the time. Lvivites hiding in churches near Lviv were found and killed. Khmelnytskyi took the High Castle but did not enter the city, opting for a ransom payment instead.

Between the 18th and the 19th centuries, the Jesuit church was used for meetings of the Galician Sejm.

During Soviet times, the cathedral was used as book depository for the Vasyl Stefanyk research library. Significant damage was caused to the church's murals and other components of its interior.

In 2011 the church was transferred to the Ukrainian Catholic Church and named the Sts. Peter and Paul Garrison. It is subject to the Center of Military Chaplaincy. Restoration of the Church continues.

51

Maria Zankovetska Theatre

This theatre was established in the mid-19ᵗʰ century. At the time, it was one of the three largest theatres in Europe. Even today, its sheer size surprises most visitors

The Lviv City Theatre was originally located in the former Franciscan Cathedral. But between 1820 and 1830, the church building and its interior began to deteriorate and it was unable to house a growing numbers of theatre-goers. The decision was made to build a large theatre at the site of the dismantled Lower Castle. Apparently, some of the bricks from the castle were used to build the theatre.

The construction of the new theatre was sponsored by philanthropist Count Stanislaw Skarbek, and thus, for decades this theatre was known as 'The Skarbek Theatre'. Skarbek instructed architects Ludwig Pichl and Johann Salzmann to design an ultramodern theatre. Once completed, the building occupied the whole quarter.

Театр трафа С.Скарбека у Львові
1836   1842

During the annual city fair, the so-called 'Kontrakty', the theatre hosted *grand balls*. Members of the local elite used these balls as an opportunity to find a spouse

It was planned that the theatre would include a stage, seating for 1460 people, theatre rooms, and also shops, a bakery, a sweet shop, a banquet hall, a restaurant, and even a hotel. However, the hotel was never commissioned. Instead, the well-known Lviv painters Artur Grottger and Juliusz Kossak resided and worked in the theatre's workshops. Even Count Skarbek lived there for a time.

The grand opening of the theatre took place in 1842.

During the theatre's lengthy history, stellar artists graced its stage including Ferenz List, Sarah Bernard, and Solomia Krushelnytska.

1900 marked the opening of the New Grand Theatre, now known as the Theatre of Opera and Ballet. Af-ter this, the Skarbek Theatre operated as the Philharmonic Hall. During the Interwar period — the era of the rise of the cinema industry — the theatre was known as the Atlantic Cinema.

As of 1944 — when the Zankovetska drama troupe began performing here — the theatre became known as the Maria Zankovetska Drama Theatre. It was the first Ukrainian theatre troupe created in 1917 on the initiative of Mykhailo Hrushevskyi, President of the Ukrainian Central Rada. Since then, the theatre has presented international and Ukrainian plays offering both serious dramaturgy (such as plays by Shakespeare, Lorca, and Shevchenko) and light musicals.

52

Segal House

This building is a reminder of the golden era of architectural development in Lviv, when each building was designed as its own work of art

Building #6 on Chaikovskoho Street, which belonged to Lviv lawyer Mina Segal, stands out despite being surrounded by other elegant buildings. With its large corner bay window, shaped windows, and its tower with a beautiful gable, this building is a wonderful example of early ornamental secession in Lviv. Tadeusz Obmiński designed it and it then housed luxurious rental apartments, successful banks and important institutions — just as it does today.

The city of Lviv was lucky that its period of active rebuilding took place at the beginning of the 20th century, an era of a new style in architecture, which was introduced as Art Nouveau in France, or Secession in Austria-Hungary (in particular, in Galicia). As a result, numerous beautiful structures were built in Lviv with plant-like curving lines and rich decor.

The interior of Seccession-style buildings are also worth exploring, paying attention to architectural details. Numerous decorative elements

The Segal building is located on the corner of Prospekt Shevchenka, one of Lviv's most beautiful boulevards, which was built *along the former Poltva River*. It has many interesting works of architecture, such as the present-day Prosecutor General's building on #17 Prospect Shevchenka, designed in a lovely late Secession style with elements of Neoclassicism

Lviv has entire "ensembles" of Secession architecture. One of the best preserved is an area on Bohomoltsia Street. The entire street was *completed in the course of just four years (from 1904 to 1908)* based on a general plan, which also included a small square. Of the approximately

twenty buildings, seven were designed by Ivan Levynskyi, one of the most prominent architects of Lviv's modern art period. Even today, Bohomoltsia Street seems to be a city within a city, with a unique spirit that has been preserved since the beginning of the 20th century

were preserved in the Segal building, including the stair railings, window frames and door jambs, stained glass, fireplace decorations, chandeliers and wall tapestries. They complement each other creating a harmonious atmosphere.

53

Kryva Lypa Passage

Though located in the city centre, this small street is cozy and laid back. Many Lvivites enjoy coming here to relax from the city's hustle and bustle

Found in a bit of a hidden location, you can get to the Kryva Lypa (Crooked Linden) Passage through stone entryways from either #6 Doroshenka Street or #3 Sichovykh Striltsiv.

This small street used to be known as the City Passage. It was built at the end of the 19th century by Ephraim Haussmann, owner of the nearby Grand Hotel. From the beginning, the passage was de-

signed as a place for relaxation and entertainment, and was open to the public, not just the hotel's guests. It originally housed photo studios, bookstores, and shops.

In its small central square, the passage actually does have a crooked linden tree, which is more than 150 years old. This is the only tree left of the former Botanical Gardens. There are benches around the linden tree,

At the end of the 19th century, the first public movie showing was held in the photo shop on Crooked Linden Passage (Passage Haussmann at the time)

Prior to World War II, there were at least eight commercial passages in Lviv, some rather *luxurious and covered with glass*. The majority of those passages were destroyed during the war, or neglected during Soviet times. Only one covered passage on #5 Mickiewicz Square was preserved, although it lost its original beauty. Some open-air passages have returned or are in the process of returning to their original purpose, such as Crooked Linden and Passage Andreolli, which connects Ploshcha Rynok and Teatralna Street

making it a nice place to stop for a rest on a hot day. Many students like to sit around it; in fact this is one of their favourite places.

The atmosphere in the passage is particularly lovely in the summertime, as the whole street turns into a large summer terrace.

The number of restaurants, bars and bistros here is probably the highest of any street in the city.

On a visit to Lypa (Ukrainian for "linden"), you can try food from the usual selection of restaurants in Ukraine, such as Italian pasta and wine, Japanese sushi, Ukrainian varenyky, or Georgian dishes. You can top your meal off with a beer from the Irish Pub, or coffee and traditional Galician desserts.

54

Sosnowski's Castle

House catches the eye, and there is nothing else quite like it in Lviv. If you explore the area around it, you will find other incredible buildings, though they're less noticeable from afar

The house on the corner of #50–52 Chuprynky Street was built in the style of Historicism with distinct Neo-Gothic and Neo-Roman elements. In fact, the project consists of two buildings, a private residence and a stone tenement house. They were built in 1900 for architect Jozef Sosnowski, based on his own design.

The building is decorated with a cornerstone tower, which has a Venetian-style balcony-gallery. It has also preserved its plasterwork in the entry hall, its original wall paintings, now faded with time, and the stone lion at the entry.

The Kastelivka District was designed in 1880 by architects Julian Zachariewicz and Ivan Levynskyi. It was an experiment influenced by then-modern ideas of decentralization and the

Jozef Sosnowski was not the only architect that chose Kastelivka to establish *his own home.* This district's architectural plans were indeed the best and most exclusive at that time

humanization of the development or residential buildings through their insertion into the natural environment. The project created several irregularly shaped residential quarters with villas drowning in a lush verdure of gardens. But it was only partially implemented; a whole residential quarter was developed in place of the planned gardens.

You can now see villas from the end of the 19th century next to residential stone houses from the beginning of the 20th century on the following streets: Nechuy-Levytskoho, Chuprynky, Kolberga, Kotlyarevskoho, Bohuna, Metrolohichna, and Horbachevskoho. Each building here is worthy of attention due to its interesting architectural details.

The villas are mostly constructed in the style of Historicism, specifically its Romantic branch. Elements of Ukrainian and Polish folk architecture, and medieval motifs are also used here. Residential apartment buildings are decorated with numerous examples of Ornamental Secession.

Each villa in the Kastelivka area was designed *completely individually*, and many embodied the latest trends in comfort and planning of the 19th century. Though it might seem incredible, many of those standards are still considered modern today

55

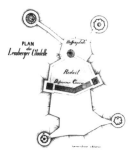

Citadel

Those who are disappointed with the absence of a real fortress on the Lviv High Castle Hill might be pleased to know there is one not too far away. They can go just over a kilometre southwest of the castle to find the Citadel

The Citadel is much younger than the High Castle but it is also an interesting and picturesque fortress, located at the top of another hill, very close to downtown Lviv. It was commissioned by the Austro-Hungarian leaders after the revolution of 1848, when the empire's power had somewhat weakened and there was a need to fortify its borders.

The Citadel complex consists of six bastions and a building with military barracks. In the 1860s and 1870s, many trees were planted on the hillsides around the fortress to hide the movement of troops. As a result, nowadays the Citadel looks like a somewhat neglected park with brick fortifications.

There is an extensive network of *catacombs under the fortress structures*. Some of them were used as bomb shelters during World War II. Here and there you can see entry points and ventilation shafts, which are indicative of the underground utility systems. They have barely been studied so far

The hill on which the Citadel is situated is sometimes referred to as Kalicha Hora (Crippled Hill). This name comes *from the hospital that was once located here.* The street that leads to the Citadel from the city centre also bears the name Kalicha Hora Street. Several other streets, like Kotsiubynski and Hrabovskyi Street also lead to the Citadel. Apparently there are a few other "secret" ways to get to the fortress which can be discovered if you have time to explore the area

There are plans to construct an entertainment complex including restaurants and clubs on the territory of the Citadel. Some civil society organizations and many Lvivites are opposed to this plan, as they believe that the *fortress should become a place of commemoration to the victims who perished here*

Despite the absolute quiet and peacefulness that reigns in this area, it is a place where very tragic events occurred. During World War II, it was where the Nazis organized the so-called "Stalag-328" concentration camp for prisoners of war, mostly from the Soviet Union and Italy. In total, the Nazis kept approximately 300 thousand prisoners here, nearly half of whom were killed.

The former military barracks are currently occupied by a bank. One of the fortress' bastions houses a book depository of the Research Library and another one has been turned into a 5-star hotel — the Citadel Inn. The rest of the bastions are abandoned. You can get to the hotel from the city centre by walking up the steep stairs through the park. Once you get to the top you will have a marvelous view of the city from the observation platform behind the hotel.

56

Lychakiv Cemetery

The history of Lviv is carved in this cemetery's stones

The Lychakiv cemetery is the oldest operating burial ground in the city. It was created in 1786 following a ban on burials in church graveyards.

Today, this cemetery is not only a place of eternal rest for the deceased, nor is it just a landscaped park with beautiful old trees and well-arranged alleys. It is also like an open-air museum of memorial sculptures and architecture.

The oldest gravestone here dates back to the 17th century, though there are few gravestones from that time. Only a small number — that date back to before the mid-19th century — have survived to this day. This is due to the installment of a stone crusher at that time, and the decision to crush any gravestones

that nobody had taken care of for more than 25 years. The crushed stones were used to pave the cemetery's alleys.

There are more than three hundred thousand graves at this cemetery. Many of the crypts and tombstones are true works of art, such as the sculpture on the gravestone of actress Regina Markovska (known as "Sleeping Beauty"). Also noteworthy is the tombstone of the Armenian archbishop Stefanovych featuring elements of traditional Armenian sacral architecture.

You can trace the history of Lviv and Galicia by the names of those buried at the cemetery. Most of Lviv's outstanding politicians, scientists, writers and artists rest in peace here.

Today, Lychakiv cemetery is not only a graveyard, but also *an official museum*. You can order a tour on the cemetery's website at www. lviv-lychakiv.ukrain. travel

As with any old graveyard, the Lychakiv cemetery has its own legends. The most romantic is a story about the *Polish artist Artur Grottger and his fiancé Wanda Monné*. They never married due to the artist's illness and subsequent death in France. Monné sold all her jewellery and a part of her dowry to bring her beloved one back to Lviv to bury him in the Lychakiv cemetery in accordance with his will. Legend has it that the ghosts of Artur and Wanda can sometimes be seen wandering in the moonlight

Lviv's multicultural heritage is felt even at this cemetery, where you can find Polish, Ukrainian, German and Armenian names on the tombstones.

Even to this day, the most prominent residents of Lviv are buried in Lychakiv cemetery; however, nowadays this is quite rare.

57

Shevchenkivskyi Hai

Lviv's picturesque open-air museum among groves and hills

The idea to create an outdoor museum of centuries-old folk architecture arose in the 1930s when Metropolitan Andrey Sheptytskyi arranged for a wooden church to be brought to Lviv from the Carpathians. It was decided it would be placed in a small forest near the "Professor's Colony" residential quarter. That was how the museum began.

The location chosen for the museum was a spot to which Emperor Franz Joseph I took a liking during one of his visits to Lviv. That is why this hilly, wooded area that is just a short distance from the city centre is still often referred to as 'Kaiserwald', or 'Emperor's Forest' in German.

In the beginning of the 1970s, the city's authorities decided to take on this project seriously and began to

The 18ᵗʰ century St. Nicholas's Church, from which the creation of the museum began, still holds masses. It belongs to the Ukrainian Greek Catholic Church and today is called *the Church of the Wisdom of God*. A small choir sings ancient Ukrainian religious chants during liturgies

Ethnography festivals, concerts, workshops, exhibitions, and other events are held at Shevchenkivskyi Hai on a regular basis. At Christmas and Easter the museum is full of people and life. It is also a favourite destination for filmmakers and newlyweds. Website: *en.lvivskansen.org*

develop the museum in the form of an ethnography park. They decided to name it "Shevchenkivskyi Hai" (Shevchenko Grove) in honour of the most outstanding Ukrainian poet — Taras Shevchenko.

Today you can see more than 120 monuments of folk architecture at the museum, representing different regions of Western Ukraine. The museum actually consists of several small villages, each with about a dozen mostly wooden structures, including churches, houses, and workshops.

A trip to Shevchenkivskyi Hai provides a relaxing break from city life. The natural surroundings allow you to imagine yourself on a trip to the mountains, while the ancient architecture transports you several hundred years back in time.

58

Holy Trinity Church

On the outskirts of Lviv, right in the middle of a Soviet-era residential neighbourhood, stands an ancient wooden church. It is practically the only reminder of the former village Sykhiv

Holy Trinity Church was built in 1654 in the tradition of Ukrainian sacral wooden architecture. There are fewer and fewer such landmarks today. That makes this particular church, which has preserved its authentic look and remained fully operational, even more valuable.

Inside, the wooden church walls are fully covered with a mural, which was rare for Galician church-es. The mural dates back to 1683, and has only been partially restored. You can find the church at #1a Sadybna St.

The first mention of the village of Sykhiv dates back to 1409. It was re-sold multiple times, but in the 16th century Sykhiv and the neighbour-ing village of Zubra were acquired by Lviv city council members. For centuries, the rural holdings provid-ed income to the city's burgomaster

*Left: **Interior decoration** of the Holy Trinity Church*

Sykhiv's main church, *the Church of the Nativity of the Most Blessed Mother of God*, is the complete opposite of the ancient wooden church. It is one of the best examples of modern sacral architecture in Lviv. In 2001, during Pope John Paul II's visit to Lviv, it was there that he met with the church's youth, at an event attended by half a million young people

The Sykhiv residential district is *the furthest from Lviv's city centre* and is separated from the main part of the city by a large undeveloped area.

Thus, in the years after New Sykhiv's development was completed, many Lvivites still treated this district as a neighbouring village. As with most rural areas, there was only one bus you could take to get there. Even now, many Lvivites feel that Sykhiv is "not quite Lviv"

(mayor) and council members.

In 1962, Sykhiv was incorporated into Lviv and the construction of industrial enterprises and multi-storied apartment buildings began there. In the 1980s and 1990s, the "New Sykhiv" district quickly developed. It is the largest residential district in Lviv, constructed for 120 thousand residents, and it consists of hundreds of similar nine-storied apartment buildings made of concrete panels. This was a standard of urban planning throughout the USSR, at the time.

NATURE

59

The Poltva

Lvivites often say that the only thing missing in Lviv is a river. The city did used to have one though, flowing right through the centre

If you look at pictures of Lviv from the 18th and 19th centuries, you will see a full-flowing river going right through the middle of today's Shevchenko and Svoboda Avenues, with an embankment stretching along it and a few bridges. This was the Poltva River.

In the late Middle Ages, the river was navigable. Fishing boats from as far away as the Baltic Sea would ply the river. Over the years it became shallower, yet back in the 19th century it still caused significant floods.

In the area of today's Mickiewicz Square, the Poltva even used to create a small island.

Boggy soil caused by the river posed an even more serious problem than floods. The washed-out ground led to the gradual destruction of the buildings standing on the river banks. This is what happened to the Low Castle, which had been located on the right bank of the Poltva River prior to the beginning of the 19th century.

The city residents also complained about swarms of mosquitoes

It is not surprising that a restaurant in the basement of the opera house is called the "*Left Bank*". The claim is true, as the left bank of the Poltva River flows right beneath the theatre. They say that sometimes from the orchestra pit of the opera house you can acutally hear the river flowing

Some people have created plans to *uncover the Poltva River and construct a modern embankment and bridges.* Implementation is a long way off, however, and at the moment not everyone agrees with the idea

and an unhealthy climate in the city, attributing all these troubles to the river.

The decision was made to cover over the Poltva, routing the river through the city sewer system. In this way they also resolved the problem of waste water disposal. The first parts of the river were covered back in the first half of the 19th century. The portion of the river flowing through the central part of the city was covered in the 1920s.

So, as you walk down Svoboda Avenue or Mickiewicz Square, be aware that right under your feet, at a depth of 3-4 meters, the Poltva River flows.

The Poltva flows out from under the ground in the northern outskirts of Lviv. There it flows through the sewage treatment facilities and then, tens of kilometres further along, it flows into the Western Bug River.

60

Ivana Franka Park

This "mini park" is much loved as it is one of
the coziest green islands in the centre of Lviv
and the oldest public park in all of Ukraine

This park, named in honour of the
well-known Lviv writer Ivan Franko,
was founded at the end of the 16th
century by the wealthy Lviv resident
Melchior Scholtz-Wolfowitz. His
son-in-law, the Venetian-born Anto-
nio Massari, designed it according to
Italian traditions, and then donated
it to the city.

Some Lvivites still refer to the
park as the 'Jesuits' Garden', since
the Jesuits owned it for almost
a hundred and fifty years. They
made use of it in their own peculiar way, by building a brickyard,
a brewery, and a tavern. Some parts

were used for agricultural purposes.
If not for the Austrian authorities,
who denied the Jesuits their title to
the land, the park might not have
survived at all.

The park was rebuilt twice more:
once, according to the French
(well-ordered) tradition, in the late
18th and early 19th century, and a second time, according to the English
(wild) tradition, in the mid-19th century. The 'French' park was a place
for merry entertainment. There was
a casino, a pool, and a special platform for fireworks. However, with
time it was ruined by small under-

Left: **Flower-bed featuring portrait of Ivan Franko** *in the park opposite Ivan Franko university, 1950–1955*

The oldest building in the park is the round gazebo that was preserved from the days of the French-style park, from the beginning of the 19th century. There used to be three such gazebos. In the 1950s, brass bands used to play here

In winter, the main path often turns into a sled path for children. Sometimes sledders travel down the hill at high speeds, so *passers-by need to be very careful*

ground springs that waterlogged it.

The park has remained in the English style until the present day, with an irregular shape and paths mirroring the landscape. It is a nice place for walks and for sitting on the benches of the main alley or its more remote paths. Among the trees growing here are magnolias, yew-trees, velvet sumach, and white-wood. Some trees are more than three hundred years old.

During Soviet times, the park was named after Ivan Franko, just like the Lviv University that stands next to it. Due to the university being so close, there are always many students in the park.

61

Lviv Weather

In Lviv they say, "hope for sun, but prepare for rain". And true Lvivites know never to leave home without an umbrella

Lviv has long had a reputation of being a rainy city. Some like to call Lviv 'the Ukrainian London'. Rain has been an almost permanent feature of many major events, and this has been noted for ages.

For example, the Galician Provincial Exhibition of 1894 saw rain on 100 of 139 days. At the end of the 18th century, when a Summer Theatre was built in Lviv, it became almost immediately necessary to build a convertible roof that would protect the audience from rain. Galicians had to develop know-how for complicated constructions like this.

Out of all of Ukraine's large cities, Lviv has the most precipitation. In total, it rains (or snows) an average of nearly half of all the days in the year. The wettest season is summer, with July being the wettest month. Nature seems to have played a joke on Lviv: despite Lviv having a "seaside" climate, residents have had frequent shortages of water. On balance,

Lviv is located on the main European watershed separating the Baltic and the Black Sea basin rivers. It is a ridge of tall hills from which natural streams flow downwards in all directions. This explains the shortage of water reservoirs. The city is *approximately 300 metres above sea level* — the highest altitude of any of Ukraine's big cities

winters are relatively mild and summers are never too hot.

Lviv weather is not only rainy and damp, it is also very un-predictable. The morning sun may change to rain in the second half of the day, and vice versa. This is why a typical Lvivite will not leave home without being equipped with both sunglasses and an umbrella.

One of the well-known jokes about Lviv weather:
— What is the weather like in Lviv?
— It's been raining.
— For how long?
— Since 1256

62

Stryiskyi Park

Spread out over picturesque hills, this is the best-known park in Lviv. Its huge trees, serpentine trails, classical alleys and romantic corners make it a favourite spot of many Lvivites

Stryiskyi Park was founded in 1879. Because of sand dunes and gulleys, it was difficult to put up any buildings here, but the area was great for romantic walks. Lviv's head landscape gardener, Arnold Röhring, carefully planned the park and planted over 40,000 trees, including exotic ones such as tulip trees, ginkgo and red oaks. Some of these trees are still growing in the park.

In 1894, the biggest industrial exhibition in the history of Galicia, the Provincial Exhibition, took place on the empty lands adjacent to the park. It involved all industries in the province, and over a million people visited it during the four months of its operation. Dozens of exhibition pavilions, a cable railroad and even a working model of an ozocerite mine

When Stryiskyi Park was first being constructed, the Polish municipal administration was looking for a place to put a monument to *Tadeusz Kilinski*, a Polish insurgent of the late 18th century. They chose the park, and this monument is still standing there today, one of few that has managed to survive the Soviet era. However, not many Lvivites would be able to tell you who this monument depicts

were constructed. Eventually, this territory was incorporated into the park.

In the interwar period, an exhibition of *Oriental Trades* was held annually on the site of the Provincial Exhibition. A dedicated narrow-gauge railway was constructed for it. Today a part of this railway has become a children's attraction, with brightly painted cars in the southern end of the park travelling between two stations, Park Station and Sun Station.

In the warmer months, mountain bikers love to cycle in the park, while in winter downhill sledding is a popular activity. A greenhouse from the earliest days of the park has been restored, there is a swan pond in the lower part of the park, and a cinema and library in the upper part.

Since the time of the Provincial Exhibition, only one pavilion, the pavilion of arts, has remained unchanged. Luckily, it is the most beautiful, and it now houses one of the *Lviv Polytechnic campus buildings*. Another building that has survived to this day is the picturesque pseudo-Gothic water tower

63

The Dove and Pigeon Market

Each Sunday the area at the intersection of Kleparivska and Zolota Streets is filled with the flutter of wings and the sounds of cooing

The doves here are mostly sold by middle-aged men, who demonstrate their birds' accomplishments by letting them fly freely and waiting for them to come back.

The sellers complain that commerce is bad at the moment, unlike in the good old days. There are fewer dove and pigeon enthusiasts, and many people buy birds online, thinking it will be cheaper and easier. But prices are actually as cheap as can be in the market: a pair of Ukrainian post pigeons goes for about $3.50, while foreign birds cost slightly more. There are white, gray and mottled birds for sale, of all sizes and breeds.

If you want to make it for trading hours, you will have to be on time. Sales begin on Sundays at 9 a.m., and by 11, sellers begin to pack up their goods. Many travel from far away, sometimes 50 to 70 km from Lviv. For them the market is not just about money, but also provides a chance to hang out with like-minded people. In a way, the dove and pigeon market on Kleparivska is an informal club for enthusiasts.

Lviv's dove market operates next to the largest and most popular "Krakivskyi" market. One can buy almost anything there, and for a good price. This market is located in the *middle of one of the pre-war Jewish residential quarters*, and partially covers an old Jewish cemetery that was destroyed by the Nazis and Soviet authorities. Next to the market is the former Jewish hospital, one of the most interesting architectural pieces in this quarter, on #8 Rappoporta Street

64

Znesinnia Park

Lviv's largest park is appreciated for its abundance of educational and recreational activities

Officially known as Znesinnia Regional Landscape Park, this is Lviv's largest park. It is only 20 minutes walking distance from the city centre, and is a favourite place for family outings. One of the city's most popular ropes courses called "LaZanka" is located in the park.

The park itself covers a total area of 312 hectares and includes the territory of the High Castle, Shevchenkivskyi Hai Open Air Museum, a residential area, an industrial zone, a cemetery and more. Wandering around the area of the park, you might come across objects of historical and cultural importance, as well as rare species of plants, all of which are protected.

In accordance with Ukrainian legislation on protected areas, the park provides environmental education and conservation.

Lviv's earliest settlements were located on the present day territory of the park, one dating back to the *Neolithic period*. Religious remnants from pagan times were also found here

In 2009, Lviv's *first indoor skateboard park* was built on the territory of Znesinnya park

SPORTS

LEOPOLIS GRAND PRIX
☎ (050) 370 02 56   НОМЕРНІ ЗНАКИ   ☎ (067) 254 32 03
2013

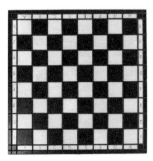

65

Vasyl Ivanchuk

The best Ukrainian chess player of all time,
Vasyl Ivanchuk is considered a chess genius

Vasyl Ivanchuk (born in 1969) is an international grandmaster, vice world champion (2002) and European champion (2004), as well as four-time winner of the chess Olympiad. For more than 20 years he was consistently among the top ten chess players in the world and was ranked No. 2 on the official FIDE rating list in 2007.

His father, a lawyer by training, taught him to play chess. Vasyl Ivanchuk grew up in the provincial town of Berezhany near Ternopil, where he had neither decent coaches nor rivals. But at the young age of sixteen, he won the Soviet Union Junior Chess Championship.

He received his "formal" chess education at the Lviv Sports University and in 1988 he demonstrated outstanding results in the New York Open. Commenting on the event, *The New York*

Ivanchuk has an uncanny memory, speaks five languages, reads widely in philosophy and, unlike many other grandmasters, *never plays chess with a computer.* However, he gladly plays with amateur chess players in the park

Ukrainian National Championship, November 2014, Lviv, Ukraine

Times called him a rising star of Soviet chess.

During the next few decades, Ivanchuk consistently won super tournaments throughout the world — from Canada and Cuba to China and the Philippines. He won first place three times at the international chess tournament in the Spanish city of Linares, which annually brings together the best chess players in the world.

Today, Vasyl Ivanchuk combines participation in international tournaments with coaching and lecturing. He also established the Vasyl Ivanchuk Chess School in Lviv, where dozens of young chess players hone their skills and participate in an annual championship. The school's website is shkolaivanchuka.com.ua

Ivanchuk's nickname in the international community of chess players is *"Big Chucky"*

66

Leopolis Grand Prix

Once a year, retro cars take to the streets of Lviv to show off their exclusive designs. The event is equally anticipated by car collectors, fans of vintage fashion, photographers, and children

The first circuit car races took place in Lviv in 1930. The track they used was in the shape of a triangle with blunt angles, and it soon became known as the 'Lviv Triangle.'

The track is over three kilometres long and is considered to be one of the most challenging tracks in Europe. This is due to its cobblestone pavement, tram rails and the steep descent of one of the streets the track crosses.

The Lviv races acquired international status in 1931 and one year later they became a part of the Grand Prix series, which was the predecessor to Formula 1. It was the only race in the Grand Prix series that was named after the track's city rather than country. Many motorcar racing stars of the time partici-

In pre-war times, the tram rails on the Leopolis Grand Prix track were filled with plaster and sand bags were placed *along the edges of the sidewalks*

Website: *www. leopolis-grand-prix.com*

pated in Lviv races, such as Hans Stuck and Rudolf Caracciola from Germany, Pierre Veyron from France and Renato Balestrero from Italy.

In 1934, the Leopolis Grand Prix was canceled because of the worsening international political situation and economic crisis.

In June 2011, the car racing tradition was resumed in Lviv in the form of 'retro races'. Today's Leopolis Grand Prix is a mix of sport, history and art. Dozens of retro cars participate each year, some of which are more than 100 years old. The racetrack is the exact same 'Lviv Triangle' that was used previously, not having changed since the pre-war period.

The present-day retro races feature bright car parades, with the participating cars cruising through the centre of Lviv. There is also a *car fashion competition*, with crews posing in clothes of the epoch represented by their cars. There is a special award for the most exquisite car

67

FC Karpaty Lviv

FC Karpaty is Lviv's best and most famous
football team

Some claim that the history of both Ukrainian and Polish football began in Lviv. It was during the State Exhibition of 1894
in Stryiskyi Park that the Lviv and Krakow teams played each
other for the first time. It was the first recorded match on the
territory of modern Ukraine, although both teams were Polish.
Hardly any rules were applied and the match lasted only seven
minutes, until the first goal was scored by a member of the
Lviv team. It is considered the first victory of a Lviv football
team.

    During the inter-war years, several strong teams played in
Lviv. They were based on ethnicity and included three Polish

There were *no
independent
football teams
during Soviet
times*, so initially
the Karpaty were
sponsored by the
Electron TV-making
plant. Later the
team and the
stadium were given
to the city of Lviv
by Electron

teams, one Ukrainian team and one Jewish team.

New chapter in Lviv football began when the Karpaty team was founded. It was created as a team where the best footballers in Lviv would play.

The team grew and improved, and in 1969 it achieved something nearly impossible — without having a higher league status, the Karpaty won the Soviet Union Cup — an unprecedented victory. The win took the team into the international arena, representing the Soviet Union during the 1970/71 UEFA Cup Winners Cup, and then — to the Soviet Top League. Full credit for all of these victories goes to Ernest Just, the team's talented coach.

During the last two decades, the team has been a part of the Ukrainian Premier League, and among the best Ukrainian football teams. FC Karpaty compete in the UEFA Europa League, albeit with variable success.

When Karpaty players are not playing well, their fans traditionally shout, *"Vivtsi! Vivtsi" (which means "Sheep! Sheep!")* This pejorative is a unique term used by Lviv fans which you won't hear anywhere else in Ukraine

68

The SKA Velodrome

This unique sheltered bicycle track
is the only one of its kind in Ukraine

The SKA Velodrome was opened in 1980 as part of the larger
sports complex of the Ministry of Defense. SKA stands for Army
Sports Club. The track has a huge wooden covering made of
Siberian larch, brought to Lviv from the Russian Far East. The
stands may accommodate up to 3,000 spectators.

Athletes and cyclists, including members of the Ukrainian
national team, train on the race track on a daily basis. Training for other sports such as athletics, boxing, archery and the
pentathlon also takes place here.

The velodrome is also used by amateurs for training and
competitions. The Insane Rover is an annual competition for
cycling enthusiasts. Rock concerts and other public events are
often held at the bicycle track because of its ample size.

The Lviv velodrome is also interesting from an architectural
standpoint, as an example of the Soviet era's functionalism.
Take note of the remarkable mosaic on the outside wall depict-
ing various athletes: a cyclist, a weightlifter and a runner.

Lvivites were among the pioneers of the cycling movement in Europe. As early as 1886, the first bike rental spot operated from the restaurant at the High Castle.

At the end of the 19th century, *a 400-metre circular track* for cyclists was constructed in Lviv. It was the predecessor of today's cycle track

The outstanding Ukrainian cyclist Tamara Poliakova (born 1960) lives in Lviv. She is a *two-time World Champion* of road bicycle racing, and

a Tour de France winner. Now she is the vice head teacher at a local sports school

Soviet cities were not designed for cycling. However, Lviv has recently undertaken some initiatives to make the city more bike-friendly. Bike paths and bicycle

parking spots are being installed, and the first Ukrainian municipal bicycle rental service, *Nextbike*, was recently launched

TECHNOLOGY

69

The Kerosene Lamp

At the beginning of the 20th century, there was a kerosene lamp in each and every house; today this fuel is still used in jet engines. Kerosene was actually invented in one of Lviv's pharmacies

In the middle of the 19th century, Galicia became an oil-producing region. Because of the affordability of oil, the owner of the Lviv pharmacy Under the Gold Star, located on #1 Kopernyka Street, decided to make alcohol out of oil. In 1853, he gave this task to his two pharmacists, Jan Zech and Ignacy Łukasiewicz.

They worked for several months

but failed to obtain alcohol from oil. They were successful, however, in producing a liquid that burnt well and had a bearable odour — kerosene. That same year, 1853, the pharmacists patented their invention in Vienna.

Zech and Lukasiewicz ordered a local tinsmith to make a lamp with a kerosene tank that they exhibited in the pharmacy window. But for

Jan Zech (1817–1897) — *pioneer of the Galician oil industry*

Before kerosene was invented, street lanterns were not only dim but also unsafe, because they used oil which often dripped and *could burn someone's skin or damage their clothes*

Before the successful experiment by the Lviv pharmacists, the liquid called kerosene had been obtained in the USA *from coal*. But this production technique turned out to be unprofitable and was not developed further

some reason, Lvivites were not interested in this new type of lamp.

Unexpectedly, it was medical doctors who helped to promote the invention. In the Lviv city hospital they performed emergency surgery by the light of kerosene lamps, which were much brighter than candles. Thus, they proved that kerosene was not only effective but also hygienic.

Jan Zech opened a shop on Krakivska Street where he sold kerosene, but the ending of this story is sad. Shortly after opening the store, some spilled fuel accidentally ignited, leading to the tragic death of the inventor's wife and sister who worked in the shop.

The more successful businessman, Ignacy Łukasiewicz, moved to Poland where he built an oil refinery.

70

The Pharmacy Museum

Under the Black Eagle on Drukarska Street is the oldest operating pharmacy in Ukraine. It is now a pharmaceutical museum, but still sells both traditional and modern medicine

Over the course of many centuries in Lviv, competition existed between the monastery and the regular town pharmacies. Monks sold medicine at lower prices and taught pharmaceutical arts to any interested individuals, not hiding their recipes. At the same time, secular shop pharmacists demanded a monopoly. This situation lasted until the Austrian government took over in Lviv.

Regardless of the risk, in 1735 a German pharmacist called Franz Natorp opened a private pharmacy in a stone building near Ploshcha Rynok. All the medicine sold there was prepared directly in the pharmacy, as was required at the time.

A legendary Ukrainian drink, *iron wine (iron saccarate) was first sold in Under the Black Eagle*. The drink, said to increase human stamina and health, is still available at the pharmacy today

Today you can still find about *ten phramacies* with historic interiors operating in the centre of Lviv

The pharmacy changed owners many times over the next 200 years, and during Soviet times it became state-owned and continued to operate.

In the 1960s, the decision was made to open a Pharmaceutical Museum on the premises of the pharmacy. Today its different rooms and halls, which you may tour, contain more than 5000 items including an ancient weighting device, pharmaceutical dishes, a large library of books on pharmacy and alchemy, and samples of medicine, including teriak — a rare universal antidote.

An alchemy lab was recreated based on old etchings. In addition to the goods, it presents materials for chemical experiments there.

In the 1980s, it was decided to restore the historical appearance of the building to the way it would have looked in the 16th century, prior to the opening of the pharmacy. The authentic-looking window panes are small and non-transparent, an effect created by using the glass-making techniques of the time.

Near the pharmacy at #2 Ploshcha Rynok is another interesting attraction, a postal museum. It is located in the 16th century building, which once belonged to Italian **Roberto Bandinelli**, who opened the first post office in Galicia

Pharmacies operating in the beginning of the 20th century were different from today in that they served as social clubs, in a sense. In **Under the Black Eagle**, the town's bohemians used to have tea or coffee, read newspapers or play cards

71

Ivan Levynskyi

At the turn of the 20th century, this man changed the architectural face of Lviv

Ivan Levynskyi (1851–1919) was an architect, engineer and successful industrialist who created the largest construction factory in Galicia, an actual 'architectural empire'. It all started with a small construction materials shop that Levynskyi opened on the outskirts of Lviv, in Kastelivka. He purchased it together with his colleague Julian Zachariewicz, also an architect.

Business went well, and soon Levynskyi had created his first enterprise — a ceramic tile factory. It was a three-story building (located today at #58 Chuprynky Street) with kilns for firing tiles, dishes and ceramic building decor.

Gradually, Levynskyi branched out his business and workshops, to include wood processing and the production of majolica, bricks and roof tiles. At his factory they also invented and patented new methods of producing gypsum and artificial stone. When they started, there were 25 workers at the factory, but just twenty years later that number had risen to 800.

In designing tiles and other household ceramics, Levyn-

*Top: Tiles intended to decorate accommodations for the **Levinskyi factory employees***

skyi used Western European styles and motifs together with Ukrainian folk ornamentation. He had the brilliant idea of inviting local architects, artists and sculptors to collaborate in his factory business. Decades after its founding, the Levynskyi factory had become an influential centre for architecture and design in Galicia, a strong competitor to those in Prague and Vienna.

Levynskyi played an even more important role for Lviv and Galicia as an architect. In creating his architectural designs, he used elements of Ukrainian modern art, which combined Western European modern traditions with Ukrainian baroque and the principles of old household and church construction. Levynskyi designed the building of the Dniester credit association at #20 Ruska Street — the most well-known structure in Lviv incorporating this style. There are many more of Levynskyi's buildings in Lviv, including public houses, villas and and multi-storied residential buildings.

Items manufactured by Levynskyi's factory can still be found today on numerous Lviv buildings, including *tiled entrances, furnaces and bricks*. They often bear the characteristic inscription "J. Lewinski i Sp." (in the Polish spelling of his name)

72

Lviv Polytechnic National University

This is the oldest and one of the largest higher technical schools in Ukraine and Eastern Europe. The academic buildings of the Polytechnic—32 in total—are spread all over the city

The Lviv Polytechnic grew out of a small Technical Academy founded in 1844 in a picturesque area of town that used to be a suburb. The Austrian authorities in Galicia had plans to make Lviv a European centre for technical education. So, in 1877 they created the Higher Technical School on the premises of the Academy.

The main building of the Technical School, located at #12 Bandery Street, was designed by the well-known Lviv architect Julian Zachariewicz. He also developed a smaller structure to house the chemistry laboratories. The Main Campus is a grand and impressive structure marked by classical proportions and forms.

Julian Zachariewicz became the Technical School's first rector.

Not all of the Polytechnic's buildings were purpose-built. Some institutions and departments are located in former monasteries, such as the Convent of Sacred Heart located at #1 St. Yuriy Square, or the monastery at the Cathedral of St. Maria Magdalena on #10 S. Bandery Street.

More campus buildings were added both during the interwar period and in the Soviet era. Some of the ones from Soviet times exemplify modern functionality, such as the Library on #3 St. Yuriy Square. Other buildings look very industrial and do not exactly improve the appearance

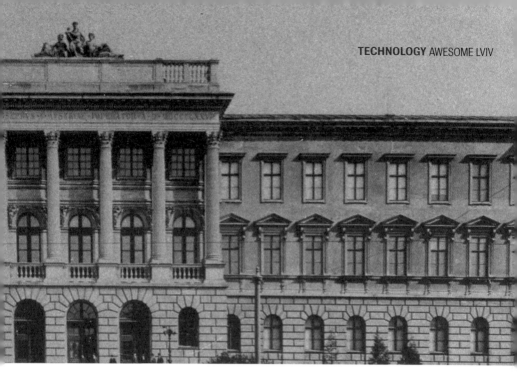

Marie Sklodowska Curie, *the world famous physician and chemist*, delivered a lecture at the Polytechnic in 1912, a year after receiving her second Nobel Prize. That day she was awarded an honorary doctorate from the Lviv Polytechnic

of the central part of the city.

Towards the end of the 19th century, the Lviv Polytechnic became one of the most important research centres in Eastern Europe in the fields of mechanical and electrical engineering and oil refining. During the interwar period, academics from the Lviv Mathematical School, together with those from the Polytechnic, started and further developed the department of functional analysis and continued the study of operations theory. The school of Architecture has a good reputation, and in recent years scholars at the Polytechnic have worked to develop innovations in energy saving technologies, information systems and telecommunications.

More than 30,000 students from 30 countries study at the Polytechnic, contributing to the multicultural flavour of Lviv.

Rudolf Weigl

The world-famous biologist and inventor of the typhus vaccine, Rudolf Weigl is often called the "Oscar Schindler of Lviv"

Rudolf Weigl was born to a family of Czech Germans, but adopted a Polish identity after his widowed mother re-married a Pole and moved to Poland. He studied at Lviv University and served as a military doctor during World War I. This experience prompted Weigl to invent the first effective vaccine against the typhus epidemic.

When World War I ended, he founded the Institute of Epidemic Typhus in Lviv. He also held mass vaccinations in China and Abyssinia at that time, saving tens of thousands of people.

During the Nazi occupation, Weigl was living in Lviv. The Nazis allowed him to further manage the Institute of Typhus on the condition that he set up production of the serum for the German Army.

Weigl was given full freedom to select his Institute staff, which provided him the opportunity to employ many Polish and Jewish intellectuals from Lviv, students and college undergraduates. This saved them

In 1948, Rudolf Weigl was nominated for the **Nobel Prize**. But the Polish Communist authorities accused him of collaboration with the Nazis, preventing him from receiving the prize

The Israeli Yad Vashem institute posthumously awarded Weigl the honorary title *"Righteous Among the Nations"*

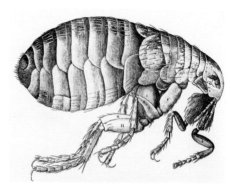

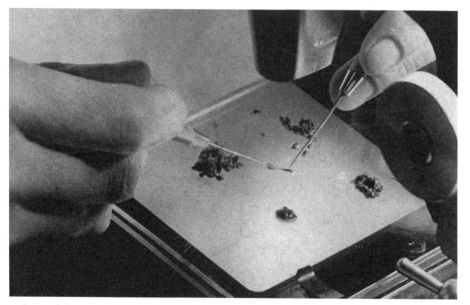

Book cover of **The Fantastic Laboratory of Dr. Weigl**, *by Arthur Allen, W.W. Norton & Co, London, 2014*
Drawing of a flea from **Micrographia**, *a book by Robert Hooke, Royal Society, London, 1665*
Lice infestation under a microscope

from unemployment and starvation, forced labour and often from death in concentration camps and Gestapo prisons.

Overall, Weigl saved approximately five thousand people during the German occupation.

74

Lviv Station Train Shed

Next time you are at the Lviv Train Station, take some time to look around. This station is an exquisite architectural landmark and a beautiful feat of engineering

The railway to Lviv was built in 1861, which was rather late by European standards, although it was the first railway station on the territory of present-day Ukraine. That first small station, with a serving capacity of just two railway lines, has since been replaced.

A new, much larger station was built at the end of the 19th and beginning of the 20th centuries, when more trains started travelling to Lviv. Plans for the new station were developed by architect Władysław Sadłowski, who designed a number of Lviv's Secession buildings. Edmund Zieleniewski, a prominent Galician engineer, also participated in the project's development and construction.

The most advanced technologies available were used in the construction of the railway station. Creating twenty pedestrian tunnels was a very

According to legend, there is a **ghost train** on the Lviv Railway. It was first seen at the end of the 19th century driving headlong towards a train from Vienna. It vanished into thin air moments before the expected collision Another progressive and technically challenging construction from the beginning of the 20th century is the "Magnus" department store, located on the corner of Horodotska and Shpytalna. It was modeled after **reinforced concrete frame** **buildings of the United States and France**. This department store, built in 1912–1913, still looks modern today

innovative idea at the time. The most remarkable part, however, was the Train Shed with its arched roof of steel and glass covering the rail tracks. The basic components of its frame were manufactured in Czech. Despite its large size, the shed seems to be weightless and made of thin lace. Lvivites were fascinated by the construction and in the beginning of the 20th century called it 'a cobweb on stems growing from concrete'.

Tragically, the shed sustained significant damage in the aftermath of the two world wars, especially after bombings in 1939. Most of the skillfully decorated components of its platforms, in particular the metal kiosks and clocks, were lost.

After World War II, the arched roof of the railway station was partially rebuilt, enough to give you the idea of the magical 'fusion of esthetics and technical perfection.'

75

Stefan Banach

This great mathematician and founder of modern functional analysis started his academic career in Lviv, where he made his most important discoveries

Stefan Banach (1892–1945) was born in Krakow. At the age of 19, he enrolled in the machine-building faculty of the Lviv Polytechnic and then transferred to engineering. Although Banach did not formally finish his studies, he was offered an assistant's position at the Polytechnic in 1920 because of his mathematical abilities. Soon after, again quite involuntarily, he defended his doctoral thesis. Apparently, his colleagues compiled some of his fragmented publications into a solid research paper and one day asked Banach to come to the Dean's office to help with a mathematical problem. There, a committee from Warsaw was waiting for him. They had a friendly talk, which in reality was the defense of his doctoral thesis. At the young age of 34, Banach became a professor of the Lviv University. His research gained international recognition in 1931 after his Polish language theory of linear operations paper was translated into French. After that, he published more than 60 important research papers.

Stefan Banach, Hugo Steinhaus, and several other Lviv mathematicians established the Lviv School

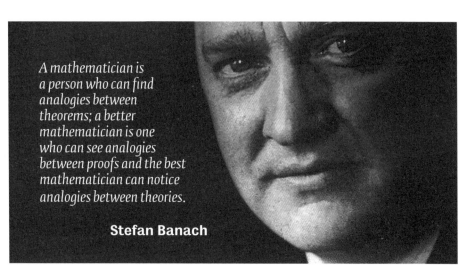

A mathematician is a person who can find analogies between theorems; a better mathematician is one who can see analogies between proofs and the best mathematician can notice analogies between theories.

Stefan Banach

Stefan Banach enjoyed *spending his time in cafes* amongst good company. But his lack of attention to financial management led him into debt, and he had to take on the low-prestige but well-paid job of writing school textbooks Many friends at the Lviv School of Mathematics and participants in their cafe discussions left their notes in the "Szkocka Book". Among them was Banach's friend, the world-famous mathematician, game theory founder and one of the fathers of the computer, *John von Neumann*

of Mathematics. It worked primarily on functional analysis, a fairly new branch at the time. The main gathering place of the group was the "Szkocka" (Scottish) cafe on #27 Prospekt Shevchenka. In the midst of highly sophisticated discussions, calculations were jotted down directly on the cafe's tabletops and later, in a notebook called the "Szkocka Book". It became a valuable scientific document and contains many as yet unsolved mathematical problems.

In 1939, Banach agreed to chair the Department of Mathematics and Physics at the Lviv University, where the language of teaching had switched to Ukrainian. He also became a member of the Municipal Council. During the Nazi occupation, when all of Lviv's universities were closed, he found shelter from persecution in Rudolf Weigl's Institute of Typhus. Like hundreds of other Lviv intellectuals at the time, he was officially employed as a lice feeder for the laboratory.

Stefan Banach died of lung cancer three days before the end of World War II.

76

The Tram Depot

Lviv's trademark trams are an intrinsic part of its atmosphere and identity. It was at the old tram depot that the history of Lviv's electric trams began

The first tram in Lviv was horse-drawn and appeared in 1880. It had three lines that connected the railway station and Pidzamche district with the city centre. But within just four years, the horse-drawn tram faced strong competition from the new electricity-powered trams.

The appearance of the electric tram coincided with the idea of holding the Provincial Industrial Exhibition in Lviv in 1894. A horse-drawn tram would never have been able to carry all of those wanting to attend the fair — more than one mil-lion people — to their destination.

The placement of the tram line and its electrification began approximately one year before the Provincial Exhibition. For the needs of the tram line, the first in-town electric power station was built, with a horsepower of 400. A tram depot was built next to it at the crossing of the streets known today as Vitovsko-ho and Sakharova.

The place selected for the power station and depot was right in the middle of the first electrified tram route connecting the main railway

Numerous traces of the former tram routes in Lviv remain to this day. They can be used to re-create an imaginary historical 'tram map' of Lviv. These include the remnants of rails and also interesting fastenings on the external walls of many buildings. Sometimes *tram cables were fastened directly to the facades*

Today, Lviv manufactures its own trams. Produced by the Electron Corporation, these trams are *modern and comfortable*

station and Stryiskyi Park, where the Provincial Exhibition was held.

By 1908, the horse-drawn tram had disappeared, but for some time its cars were still often attached to electric trams. Meanwhile, tram routes grew in number. By 1970, there was a special tourist tram line in Lviv, which went up the steep ascent to the foot of the Vysokyi Zamok.

Today the old tram depot looks almost as it had at the time of its creation. It is a beautiful example of the industrial architecture of the late XIX century. Here in the depot, the historical tram cars (the oldest dating back to the 1910s) have been restored and cared for by public organizations and volunteers.

There is a new project in the works for the re-design of the old depot. Called Creative Quarter, it would host anti-cafes, co-working spaces, a centre for child development and an eco-park. If this project goes ahead, it is very possible that a new page will soon be opened in the history of the depot.

Electron

One of the largest and oldest industrial enterprises in Lviv, "Electron" currently manufactures technologically advanced products ranging from microelectronic materials to electric transport such as trams and trolleybuses

Electron traces its history back to a small electrical engineering workshop called "Kontakt", founded in 1918 in Lviv. This work-shop developed quickly and within a decade it had turned into a factory with representative offices all over Poland and Germany.

In 1957, the Lviv Television enterprise was created based on the Kontakt factory (a Lviv measurement equipment producer at that time). That was also when the first Lviv brand TV set was produced.

The Electron Corporation is also engaged in growing *single crystals*. For the first time in Ukraine, the production of nanomaterials for electronics has been launched here

In the 1980s, one in every four Soviet TV sets was made in Lviv and by the beginning of the 1990s Electron's total output reached 15 million TV sets. Electron was the only manufacturer of television equipment that exported to Western Europe.

In the early 1990s, Electron, like most post-Soviet enterprises, faced a crisis caused by economic collapse. To survive, it had to change its production line and significantly expand its portfolio. Today, Electron is mainly a machine-building corporation. They were the first in Ukraine to launch the production of low-floor trams and trolleybuses. The number of Electron trams in Lviv is steadily increasing.

The corporation produces multifunctional municipal vehicles and off-road ambulances, and in 2015 it also produced the first electric bus in Ukraine.

In the 1980s, the company participated in the Soviet space program by producing *training simulators* for astronauts and onboard television equipment for orbital stations

78

Lviv's IT Industry

Lvivites can be proud of the many recent successes in its rapidly developing IT industry

Lviv's booming IT industry is proof that Lviv is an attractive location not only due to its historical grandeur, but also its future potential, particularly in areas of technology.

In 2009, Lviv was recognized by KPMG to be one of the most promising cities for IT outsourcing, alongside 30 other cities around the world. And in 2014, Tholons included Lviv in a list of

The Lviv IT Cluster group links IT companies with schools and local authorities. As part of a recent project called IT Future, some of the city's IT experts visit schools to hold *entertaining and informative presentations* for students in grades 9–11

the top 100 outsourcing centres.

At present, there are more than two hundred IT companies in Lviv, and nine IT training centres.

With the average IT programmer's salary being about 10 times higher than that of employees in other fields of work, it's no wonder students are flocking to obtain IT degrees.

79

Dentist Tourism

A visit to a dentist can be an expensive and painful experience, that's why a lot of people travel to see Dr. Yourko in Lviv for to have an affordable, yet professional tooth fix

As you enter Dr. Yourko's boutique dental office you will find yourself in a baroque inspired salon complete with period clocks, a candelabra and a piano. When you notice a young woman playing a Chopin nocturne you instinctively think that you are in the wrong place, but you are not. This is the workshop of a dentist who approaches his trade like an

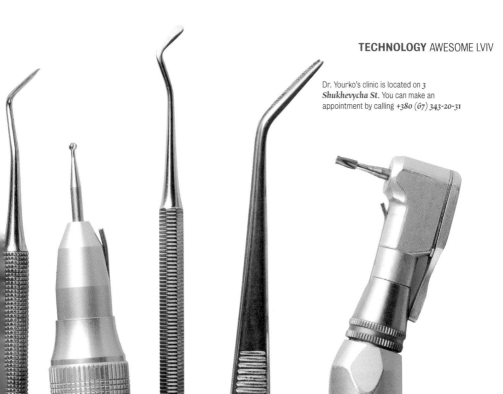

Dr. Yourko's clinic is located on 3 *Shukhevycha St.* You can make an appointment by calling +380 (67) 343-20-31

artist. He plays the piano between the appointments to recharge, and hires an accomplished performer to play while he works. "At the age of six I knew I wanted to be a dentist", says Yourko´, "it took me years to recognize my gift and to learn how to channel it. The music creates a calm relaxing atmosphere for the patients and inspires me" explains the doctor.

Dr. Yourko´ creates world class results which he guarantees for a lifetime. His unpretentious joyful demeanor would be well suited for a street juggler, yet when he starts talking his craft you instantly recognize a pedantic professional whose confidence disarms any skeptic. His patients travel from all over Ukraine, Europe and the US to see the "doctor whom they trust". "Complete trust in what I do is what creates a masterpiece smile. It's the doctor and the patient working together to come as close as possible to the ideal", that's how Dr. Yourko´ describes his medical process.

80

81

AWESOME UKRAINE App

   @AwesomeUkraine

AWESOME Series

More from Awesome Series: Awesome Ukraine,
Awesome Kyiv, Awesome Odesa. There you will find
all that we love about these Ukrainian cities — from
national dishes to historical facts, symbols, mythology,
popular culture and much more.

Awesome Dnipro and **Awesome Kharkiv** coming soon!

Order now on our website!
osnovypublishing.com